SAILING
OHANA

A Mother's Dream
A Family's Journey

REBECCA
BERGER

To request permission, contact: beckyberger@yahoo.com

Paperback: ISBN: 979-8-35092-772-6 (print)
E-book: ISBN 979-8-35092-773-3 (eBook)

Printed in U.S.A
Published by:
BookBaby
7905 N. Crescent Blvd.
Pennsauken, NJ 08110
First paperback edition: October 2023

Cover Design: Cherie Foxley, www.cheriefox.com
Map by: Ben Pease, www.peasepress.com
Illustration: Michael Cashmore-Hingley @cartoonhingers

www.beckyberger.com
www.sailingohana.com
Instagram @sailingohana

To my *Ohana,*

Paul, Madison, and Kelsey
You are and forever will be my greatest adventure.

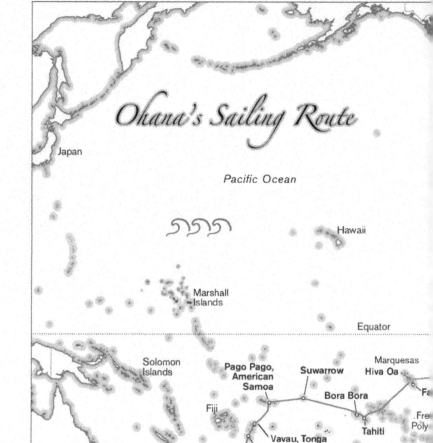

United States

Atlantic Ocean

Mexico

West Palm Beach, Florida
Key West
Nassau, Bahamas
Exumas
Isla Mujeres
Georgetown
Puerto Aventuras

Placencia, Belize
San Andreas, Colombia
Rio Dulce, Guatemala
Bay Islands, Honduras

Admiralty Bay, Galapagos

Panama City

Ecuador

Brazil

Peru

Pacific Ocean

Argentina

Chile

Atlantic Ocean

0   1000   2000 miles

0   1000   2000 km

Fear

by Kahlil Gibran

It is said that before entering the sea

a river trembles with fear.

She looks back at the path she has traveled,

from the peaks of the mountains,

the long winding road crossing forests and villages.

And in front of her,

she sees an ocean so vast,

that to enter

there seems nothing more than to disappear forever.

But there is no other way.

The river can not go back.

Nobody can go back.

To go back is impossible in existence.

The river needs to take the risk

of entering the ocean

because only then will fear disappear,

because that's where the river will know

it's not about disappearing into the ocean,

but of becoming the ocean.

Note from the Author

Over a decade has passed since we closed *Ohana*'s cockpit door for the last time.

The precious moments we lived as a traveling family from 2001 to 2012 remain etched in my memory as if it were yesterday.

As I sit typing out these words, I notice the leaves from the birch trees falling gently outside the window. They've turned a beautiful golden color after another fleeting Alaska summer. *Where does the time go?* I wonder, glancing around our quiet house. Since Kelsey and Madison have moved out and on with their own lives, I use this time to reflect, remember and write.

I struggle to find adjectives that might accurately describe our life aboard our catamaran *Ohana*. There are so many. Our travels took place before the invention of the iPhone and high-tech gadgets to document every moment. My fondest memories simply reside in my heart, bursting to share with others, including our now-adult daughters. Writing this book has been an amazing journey in itself, reliving our adventures all over again while offering a window into our seafaring world.

Many who came before us took a similar path—searching for a more fulfilling lifestyle, stronger relationships, and a greater purpose. Today these cruising families are celebrities in their own right—raising kids at sea and moving around the globe while creating incredible videos for all to enjoy. But like ourselves, they are just regular people who found a way to live their dream.

I lugged my used Canon EOS around everywhere in a sandy, wet backpack—that camera was the only means of capturing the memories. I am surprised and grateful any image survived the beating. Today, thanks to Instagram, I continue to upload photos from our nomadic life @ sailingohana. What we lacked in technology, we made up for with countless unfiltered moments, time, and attention.

Our mission was simple: to live out our dreams and passions as parents, while being fully present and involved in our children's lives. We believed that a family that plays together stays together. For us, this proved to be true.

This memoir has been a project I've put aside since we moved back to Alaska from New Zealand ten years ago. Predictably, life back on land thrust us into busyness once again—inescapable productivity that paves the way for the next big thing, whatever that may be.

Since our return, I've been encouraged to share our story—how we managed to live together on a boat for four years, plant ourselves in New Zealand for seven, and why we chose to sail away from a near perfect life in the first place. The following pages might offer a glimpse into our world, answer those questions, and may even light that spark for those who wish to live a life less ordinary as well.

No dream is too big, and everyone's story is worth telling.

This is ours.

Prologue

S ea everywhere.

The swelling waves rose and fell around our boat like the ever-present knot in my stomach as I watched the last faint outline of green disappear from the horizon. As the rumbling engines pushed our catamaran forward and further away from our beautiful island paradise, I began to question our sanity.

What are we doing; are we crazy? We can't go back! Can we go back? No, we are doing this!

The 3,000-mile passage from the Galápagos to the Marquesas lie ahead of us. Prior to our departure, many sleepless nights were spent mulling over all the things that could go wrong with a two- and five-year-old in the middle of the Pacific Ocean—falling overboard, sea sickness, pirates—the list went on.

All part of the journey, I anxiously reminded myself. *I signed up for this.*

No sooner had we motored out of Academy Bay than the water went from a clear turquoise blue to a thick, ominous black. I searched for another vessel that could be our travel companion for the next three weeks. Nothing ahead, nothing behind. Just our little family floating on the biggest body of water I'd ever seen.

Shielding my eyes from the glaring sun, I twisted my body right and left at the helm station, scanning our liquid environment now devoid of any land. Inhaling the fresh air, I mentally went over our departure list for what seemed like the hundredth time.

Customs paperwork complete . . . check. Running lights on . . . check. Girls in their cabins . . . check. I peeked through the deck hatch leading to their bunkrooms below. They were already playing with dolls together. *Fishing rods in, ditch bag out, EPIRB ready.*

Our Emergency Positioning Indicating Radio Beacon was more than just a plastic orange and yellow object secured safely on the shelf. To me, it was our connection to the outside world should something, God forbid, disastrous happen. Shaking off the thought, I continued down the list. *Watermaker on . . . check. VHF radio turned to channel 16 . . . check.*

Sailing chatter was the best chatter. Today, however, we weren't hearing any transmission. No yachties making happy-hour plans, no weather updates or chart swaps.

We've come this far, it's just a bigger ocean, we'll be fine! I reminded myself, taking a deep breath.

Glancing around the deck, I jumped off my perch, picking up the blue and red lines left tangled in the cockpit. I coiled them around my arm as I'd been taught in my offshore sailing course, tucking them neatly away in their respectful cubbies.

As the wind picked up, the waves rushing underneath our hulls had a consistent, steady rhythm. Soon we would put up our sails. There was no going back.

Dressed in my usual sailing attire—cutoff denim shorts and a faded tank top purchased from some beach bar—I returned to the helm seat. For over an hour, I studied the cresting waves and the unique shape each made before they fell away. The salty air started to cool as the sun dipped lower in the sky. A tiny light appeared inside. Paul had clicked on his desk lamp where he sat jotting notes down in his logbook.

Gazing up at the sky, I said a silent prayer as I did before every passage.

Dear God, watch over us as we make our way across your magnificent ocean. I know and trust that you will provide all we need for a safe and peaceful passage. In Jesus' name, Amen.

Kelsey hollered from below, snapping me back to reality. "Mom! Mommmm! Mommy!" Her little blonde head popped out of the hatch next to my feet. She giggled, handing me a half-dressed Barbie.

"Coming, you silly!" I laughed, bending over for a kiss.

I took one last look around, patted *Ohana's* top deck, and stepped inside.

SECTION 1

Ready

CHAPTER 1

A Girl from Alaska

"Find out who you are and do it on purpose."

—DOLLY PARTON

I grew up in an igloo.

In the winter, when our house was covered in snow, it looked like a little mound of white. It was the first geodesic dome built in Anchorage, Alaska by my dad after he and my mom drove up from Minnesota in 1962. I was always impressed by their decision to leave all they knew and drive across the country in an old pickup truck—with a few belongings and a big dream—to raise a family and begin their own journey.

Growing up in The Great Land, my two older sisters, younger brother, and I found adventure everywhere—even in our own backyard. It was the 1970s. There were no subdivisions, car dealerships or fast-food chains like those that now line the Old Seward Highway—just an old dirt road. We left the house for Taku Elementary before sunrise, sneaking through a hole in our backyard fence.

There were no iPhones or computers back then. The only screen I remember was the one on our front door that slammed shut with a creaky bang each time we came and went. Divided between the four of us, that was roughly one hundred times a day.

My mom kept her kids out of trouble by signing us up for just about every sport. When I wasn't swimming laps at the local YMCA, I was playing softball, shooting hoops or running around a track.

Our vintage TV console had only three channels, reserved for news, nature shows, and Saturday morning cartoons. Most of the time we simply got lost in our own imaginations: making up games, building forts, collecting bugs, reading, or drawing. A handful of plastic animals and a pile of dirt could keep us busy for hours.

Being third in line, I looked up to my sisters, who were talented gymnasts, and tried following in their footsteps. What I lacked in grace I made up for in grit. I gave up the beam for ball sports, fouling out of just about every basketball and soccer game. I couldn't seem to control my arms or my temper. Luckily, my love of sports through high school saved me from extracurricular distractions. Most of the time.

After graduating from Dimond High School, I enrolled at the University of Alaska, Anchorage. For two uninspiring years, I sat in sterile classrooms staring out at the bleak darkness, trying to focus on Calculus and English literature.

My best friend had chosen the University of Nevada, Las Vegas to study hospitality. She talked me into joining her. The big, modern campus in the desert promised fun, sun, and exciting opportunities. I transferred credits, bought my first airplane ticket, and moved into an apartment together on the Las Vegas strip. Jumping from one elective class to another, I discovered I had a knack for writing; a pastime I enjoyed as a child.

I declared my major in communication studies and became a reporter for the *Running Rebel* college newspaper. I loved the thrill of finding stories around campus to write about and building confidence by engaging with others.

Between a full schedule of classes, I worked as a reservation agent at The Jockey Club hotel and modeled designer clothing at Caesars Palace—anything I could do to pay rent, tuition, and still have enough left over for an occasional In-N-Out burger.

After receiving my bachelor's degree and completing a lengthy internship, I was offered a sales position at a major advertising agency. Although tempting, I was ready to turn down the bright lights and late nights of the neon strip and return home. I missed the mountains, the fresh air, and my family.

I went back to work at our local Nordstrom department store where I had been employed during high school and college breaks. Shortly after, I got an additional job in sales at KTUU, our local Channel 2 television station, eventually saving enough money to move into an apartment with my sister.

Working in advertising became monotonous and unfulfilling. Like the dark winter days, the walls of my tiny office closed in on me. I was tired of selling suits and handbags. I looked into joining YWAM (Youth With A Mission) and the Peace Corps. I wanted to feel alive, live a more purposeful life, but instead, I felt lost.

One night I lay in bed, restless, unable to sleep. Staring up at the brown water stain on the ceiling, I thought, *I can't go on living this way. Something has to change.* With tears rolling down my cheeks, I decided at that moment to do just that—change.

I walked into my boss's office at the station the next day and quit my job. I put my two-week notice in at Nordstrom. I didn't know what lay ahead, but I knew it didn't include a cubicle, deadlines, or designer shoes.

I was ready for new adventures and bigger dreams.

CHAPTER 2

A Boy and His Boat

"The only person you are destined to become is the person you decide to be."

—RALPH WALDO EMERSON

While I was busy growing up in Alaska, 4,000 miles and a world away a little boy named Paul Richard Berger was doing the same.

In the small upstate town of Fishkill, New York, Paul grew up like most boys did in the '70s—playing with friends, riding dirt bikes, and camping with his family in the Hudson River Valley.

Paul was a member of the Sea Scouts—an inclusive program offered through the Boy Scouts of America. While his growth as a sailor and young leader flourished, so did the bond between him and his father. They shared their love of boats by racing Sunfish and Lasers together on the weekends. Soon the young mariner was crewing J24 sailboats even before getting his driver's permit. The Sea Scouts gave Paul the hands-on seamanship that put him one step ahead of the rest, leading to success on and off the water.

One summer, when Paul was twelve, he and his mom, dad, and younger sister sailed up to Newport, Rhode Island. As they entered Narragansett Bay, they heard sirens. Two U.S. Coast Guard patrol boats rocketed out from the Station Castle Hill Coast Guard base. Shiny white vessels with red and blue stripes, roaring engines and blazing lights captured Paul's imagination. He decided at that moment what he wanted to do. Three years later, he dragged his dad into a recruiter's office in Poughkeepsie, New York and signed up for delayed entry into the United States Coast Guard.

The reality of an entry-level Coastie didn't match his dream. Instead of a gleaming white patrol boat, the 17-year-old recruit was stationed on an old black tug.

It was there in Narragansett Bay that Paul trained to be an electronics technician and went on to earn a First-Class FCC license with Radar Endorsement. After four years of towing buoys and breaking ice around New England, followed by drug operations in the Caribbean aboard the USCGC Bibb, he decided it was time to change course.

At 21, Paul had moved to Florida putting his technical skills to work as a broadcast engineer at WCRJ in Jacksonville, Florida, while simultaneously obtaining his 100-Ton Master Captain's License. There he managed to buy his first investment property—a small duplex on the wrong side of US 1. By renting the adjoining apartment, he achieved his goal to live for "free".

As much as he enjoyed fixing up his property and spinning country hits, the pull of the sea was relentless. He soon quit radio and made use of his newly obtained captain's license running summer charters out of Stonington, Connecticut and Newport, Rhode Island. He returned to Florida, joining a friend who had a small struggling yacht brokerage in North Palm Beach. By day, Paul worked hard selling trawlers, sportfish, and sailboats—whatever they could list. By night, he attended Palm Beach Junior College to obtain "the broadest, vaguest liberal arts degree conceivably possible."

Life felt like a hamster wheel. Paul knew what he wanted, but unsure of how to get there.

One particularly hot night after a very long day at work, he lay in bed staring at the ceiling. A single thought went through his mind.

I can't go on living this way, something has to change. Tears rolled down his cheeks. He decided at that moment to do just that—change.

The very next day he left the brokerage, put his hard-fought-for duplex on the market and sold it quickly. With just a few belongings, Paul packed up his Mazda 626 and headed north to Tallahassee, Florida to finish his undergraduate degree in International Affairs and Geography, followed by an MBA at the Maine Maritime Academy.

Penniless but fully educated, it was time for this scholar to settle down and make a living. His best friend, Armand, had moved to Alaska from Florida to look for real estate investment opportunities and encouraged Paul to do the same.

Trading his board shorts for Carhartts, Paul charged a flight on his well-worn credit card.

He was ready for new adventures and bigger dreams.

CHAPTER 3

First Mate

"Love is but the discovery of ourselves in another,
and the delight in the recognition."

—ALEXANDER SMITH

I liked him immediately.

Sporting a dark tan and mirrored Maui Jim sunglasses, Paul sauntered into my life like he was walking down a dock – confident and carefree. He had just flown into Anchorage from Palm Beach to visit his best friend and see what this new city had to offer.

Coincidentally, I had known Armand for a year prior as he was dating my sister Susie.

With twinkling eyes and a talkative, friendly nature, Paul introduced himself hugging me as if we were old friends.

"It was a blizzard outside," he describes the night we met. "You walked through the door of your sister's house in a satin blue ski jacket, dropping your fur-lined hood. Your laugh and energy immediately took my breath away."

Our coffee meetups turned into dinner and movie dates, followed by hiking, camping, and ski trips.

Armand, having a few income-producing rental properties of his own, inspired Paul to find opportunities as well should he decide to make Alaska his home. After weeks of scouting out Anchorage neighborhoods, Paul closed on a fixer-upper four-plex and quickly got to work. After months of renovations, he flew to Pennsylvania where his parents lived to collect the rest of his belongings and share his good news.

"I have found the girl I'm going to marry!"

Returning to Alaska shortly thereafter, Paul moved in with Armand, sharing a house in Eagle River, a town 30 minutes outside of Anchorage. My sister and I would drive out for weekly fireside dinners, all gathering around a big wooden table to talk about life, our dreams and ultimately planning big adventures together.

That winter, the four of us took time off from work and chartered a sailboat out of Fort Lauderdale, crossing the Gulf Stream to the Bahamas. Paul had introduced Armand to sailing in high school and both were excited to share their skills with us while exploring these beautiful islands.

Over the course of two weeks, Paul taught me how to take a chart fix, tie a Bowline knot and how to properly spear a lobster. To me, sailing felt like camping on the water. Showers were taken from a plastic bag hung from the boom, sleeping was incredibly uncomfortable, and pesky flies were everywhere—I loved it.

Lying on the foredeck together under a canopy of constellations, Paul and I talked about our goals and where we saw ourselves in ten years.

"I got to know a driven, loving, funny, inquisitive, adventurous, intelligent, warm-hearted woman who shared many of my own dreams and desires," he would tell me. "I knew someday you would be my wife."

CHAPTER 4

Tying the Knot

St. John, U.S. Virgin Islands

"Sometimes the most scenic roads in life are the detours you didn't mean to take."

—ANGELA N. BLOUNT

We had just one requirement for our ceremony—it had to be on an island.

It would take some extra cash and creativity, but we knew we could pull it off. Paul took a side job teaching geography at the university to add extra money to our wedding kitty, but mostly because he enjoyed talking about what he loved.

Meanwhile, I got a new job managing a Sylvan Technology Center. Working alone facilitating student exams gave me the time I needed to plan for our big day.

Paul continued searching for handyman specials and convinced a friend to invest in a dated twelve-plex that needed many improvements.

This building was just the beginning of what would soon become our livelihood, or as Paul called it, "our empire".

I moved out of my sister's place to share one of these apartments with him. I wasn't a fan of living together before marriage, but our wedding day was just six months away. We discovered each other's quirks, claimed our sides of the bed, and wrestled over the TV remote. From our little balcony overlooking the Sullivan Arena, we watched the fireworks display while toasting to the New Year. Paul and I spent weekends roaming garage sales to furnish our humble home.

Gatherings with friends and a couple of newly adopted kittens filled our place with warmth and laughter. As much as we loved playing house, we were anxious to be married.

We agreed on an intimate ceremony with just our immediate families and chose the U.S. Virgin Islands, a place we dreamed of sailing to one day. While everyone covered their travel expenses, we paid for the vacation rental. It was a fine-tuned plan for our guests to get to know each other and celebrate while vacationing in paradise.

A few months after we first met, a friend from Paul's yacht broker days called him about a boat he had for sale. The Hughes monohull "needed a bit of work", he warned, but the price was right. On a whim and eager to return to the water, Paul and Armand became owners of a 40-foot sailboat in need of many upgrades. After a couple trips to Florida and dozens of visits to West Marine, they brought the tired old sloop back to life.

Named after Scarlett O'Hara's, the bar they frequented back in St. Augustine, *Scarlett* was born, her hull sporting a fresh new coat of red paint.

Paul and Armand took turns managing each other's properties which allowed us time to slowly bring her down to the Virgin Islands and as my work schedule allowed. We sailed from the Bahamas to Turks and Caicos, the Dominican Republic, and finally anchoring her in beautiful Cruz Bay on the island of St. John. During these passages, we got to know each other on a much deeper level; nothing but the sea and the stars to guide us.

Night after night, by the golden glow of our lit kerosene lamp, we would talk about our life together, having kids one day and a place to call home. I fell more in love with the man I'd soon call my husband.

I quickly realized that my full-time job at Sylvan would never allow me to travel as much as we wanted. Being self-employed, Paul managed his own time and hired out work when necessary. I was the one holding us back. Quitting Sylvan, I enrolled in evening classes at Alaska Career College, receiving a certificate in airline reservations systems. I was hired as a customer service agent at Alaska Airlines the following week. Not only was I happier engaging with travelers from all over the world, but the job offered free and discounted flight benefits, which I eagerly took advantage of.

After months of working overtime, trading shifts, and saving every dollar, the day had finally arrived. I booked a luxury vacation home overlooking the bay where *Scarlett* was moored. Perched on a cliff, *The Prasanthi House* was one of the most beautiful places on Earth.

The eight-bedroom home with its breezy open-air rooms and Spanish terracotta tile flooring accommodated all ten of us—six on my side, four on Paul's.

From the villa's palatial terrace, we could see our boat's crimson hull standing out amongst the other white ones. I couldn't wait to be alone with my fiancé—I didn't care where; the world was our oyster.

The balcony, covered with fuchsia-pink bougainvillea, framed a perfect picture of swaying palms and sailboats. We all lounged in the infinity pool singing along to Jimmy Buffett songs playing from the outdoor speakers. It was everything I dreamed of.

My future mother-in-law blended margaritas for all while my mom searched the island for a wedding cake. In our rented open-air jeep, she and Paul drove around St. John returning empty-handed. We happily settled for sugar cookies.

The naive expectation that we would find an officiant once we arrived on the island proved unfruitful. All the pastors were either booked out or on holiday. Discouraged by our lack of planning, Paul and I took a lunch break in town. At the end of the tiki bar sat a jolly old man chatting with just about everyone—including us. After a couple rounds of beer, he nonchalantly shared that he was an ordained minister. We couldn't believe our luck.

"Could you marry us this weekend?" I asked hopefully, pressing my hands together.

"As long as you keep these things coming!" he grinned, holding up his drink. "I'll even take care of the flowers!"

Although a little tipsy at any hour of the day, Minister Bob was true to his word. Wearing flip-flops, a floral shirt, and a sun-faded straw hat, he strolled into *Prasanthi* as if he owned the place. In one arm he carried a large basket of fragrant tropical flowers—frangipani, bougainvillea, and bird of paradise—and in the other hand, a bottle of Red Stripe.

With a twinkle in his eye, he got right to work arranging his hand-picked flowers on the tables and railings. It was obvious he had done this before.

As the sun was setting over the bay, I took my dad's arm as he escorted me to the circular veranda. As the bridal version of Abba's "Dancing Queen" played from the speakers, I made my way next to Paul, who was framed by his father and my sister Susie. Minister Bob had changed into an oversized baby-blue suit, looking like someone who had just stepped out of an '80s prom. Paul and I stifled our laughter long enough to say our vows and "I Dos". We were finally married!

After many congratulatory hugs, we celebrated with a delicious homemade banquet of food, champagne toasts, dancing, and a late-night swim.

The next day our families joined us for a sail around the bays—Paul and I at the helm, navigating together for the first time as husband and wife.

When the last of the rum was gone, and everyone had flown back to the States, we stepped back on board, hand in hand. The world was ours—a sailboat, time, and each other.

We planned to sail to St. Croix, just 37 nautical miles away. With its white sandy beaches and surrounding coral reefs, it was close enough for all we wanted to do.

An unexpected wind shift changed our anticipated smooth sail. For the next two hours, *Scarlett* nosedived into 30-foot swells. I rarely got seasick, but this roller coaster was more than my stomach could take.

"Little squirrely out here!" Paul hollered above the noise, trimming the jib sheet. Gripping tightly to the wheel, I glanced over at him, wondering if his discomfort matched my own. He didn't seem bothered as he put a double wrap around the winch. Whenever the boat rose above every steep wave and plunged back into the sea, he'd shout, "Are we having fun yet?!" I wrinkled my face in frustration and found the direction of the wind. "Can we go *that* way?!" I yelled as seawater came sideways into the cockpit, drenching me.

Paul grabbed the charts that had slid along the cockpit table, giving them a quick study. Long black curls swept across his face. "How does Puerto Rico sound?" He shouted, chuckling at the sight of his wife, clad head to toe in foul weather gear.

We quickly jibed, turning the bow in a westerly direction towards Fajardo. The noise subsided, and we surfed effortlessly forward with each cresting wave. Wiping my eyes with a towel, I noticed Paul calculating our new arrival time.

"We'll be on the beach in no time my dear!" he said, grinning.

At that moment, I didn't even care. We were right where we were supposed to be.

CHAPTER 5

Telltales

West Indies, Lesser Antilles

"We can't direct the wind, but we can adjust the sails."

—THOMAS S. MONSON

As the snow blanketed the city of Anchorage, our minds wandered back to our warm, carefree island days. It had been seven months since our wedding, and we got right back to work, making up for the weeks playing in the Caribbean. I continued taking extra shifts at the airport and working Nordstrom sales, anything to save up for our next sailing trip. By day, Paul fixed up properties, and by night he would teach plate tectonics to a classroom of college kids. As often as we could, Paul and I would hop on a stand-by flight to the last place *Scarlett* was anchored.

Nothing was more exciting than spreading out new cruising charts wondering where to explore next. Latitude and longitude lines guided us to our next playground, while sketches of palm-fringed, horseshoe bays soon became reality.

This time it was Anguilla—an island in the Lesser Antilles with sandy beaches so fine it was like walking on clouds. I took my position at the bow seriously as we precariously navigated our way through the bommies, pointing them out as we motored through the shallowest waters. We continued to St. Martin, Barbuda, St. Kitts, and Nevis before finally settling in Antigua for a few days.

On our last evening there, we met a young couple on the dock who invited us over for happy-hour drinks. Our jaws dropped when we approached their boat at the end of the pier.

It was so big it blocked out the sun. While the owner was away during the hurricane season, these 30-year-olds were hired as caretakers to watch over and keep the vessel sparkling clean. *What a cool job,* I thought as I walked up a gleaming teak gangplank. After a grand tour we settled onto the white leather cushions surrounding the flybridge. The bird's-eye view of the entire marina showed us how small our boat looked in the distance. The couple shared how they spent their days jet-skiing, diving, and polishing brass. As the sun set, we finished off a bottle of champagne, laughing over shared stories and experiences.

"How did you get here?" they asked us. "You're so young. Do you have jobs? Is that your parents' boat?"

We chuckled and told them a little of our backstory, somewhat in disbelief ourselves.

"Wow, it really can be done!" They said, shaking their heads. After a few hours of lively conversation, Paul and I waved goodbye and happily stumbled back to *Scarlett*. As I removed our old companionway hatch door, I noticed our peeling varnish and thought of the glossy handrails on the megayacht. I smiled, thinking, *It's not about the boat but the people on it.* Cruisers were all much the same—chasing dreams, looking for adventure and like-minded friends. As I stepped inside, the familiar smell of mildew, coconut oil, and diesel filled my nose. To me, it was the scent of home.

We continued down the Windward Passage, fine-tuning our sailing skills and creative galley recipes. We learned to make honey on Nevis from the tiny island's only beekeeper. In Montserrat, we took a helicopter over an active volcano. In Dominica, a guide took us into the dense jungle to the mighty Trafalgar Falls. We rode mopeds along the cliffs in St. Lucia and eventually sailed into Grenada's Prickly Bay Marina. Wherever we went, adventures followed, and new friends were made. One such family invited us onboard their beautiful sailboat for dinner before we left the island. Halfway through my grilled fish and fried plantains, I felt a little queasy, thinking it might be the cooked bananas.

With all the instincts of a mother, Barbara looked at me, smiling, and said, "You're pregnant."

The following day as we waited for our flight back to Miami, I bought a pregnancy test at the airport chemist just for fun. I ran to the restroom, gripping the small box in my hand, surprised at how excited I felt. My friend was right. Two red parallel lines showed up as perfectly as the telltales on our sails.

We were going to have a baby!

CHAPTER 6

Motherhood

"There's no way to be a perfect mother and a million ways to be a good one."

—JILL CHURCHILL

Whatever joy I thought sailing brought me, nothing came close to being a mother. My world view changed the instant our daughter, Madison, was placed in my arms.

Even on sleepless nights when our newborn struggled to settle down, I was completely overwhelmed with an unexplainable depth of love I had never experienced before. My life was no longer about me and my own desires, but to care for and protect our daughter fiercely.

An easy and happy travel companion, "Maddi" made several trips with us to Mexico, California, Arizona, Florida, and Hawaii all before her second birthday. All she required were diapers, a baby backpack carrier, and her milk supply. Motherhood transformed me from the inside out giving me more strength, humility, confidence, and purpose than I ever thought possible.

Armand had also married and moved back to Florida with a family of his own. It was time to say goodbye to our carefree sailing days on

Scarlett and settle down. The boat was sold, and our vagabond life became a distant memory.

Paul and I moved out of the 12-plex and bought a tiny house in Spenard, a quirky neighborhood in midtown Anchorage. After a fresh coat of paint, new kitchen, carpet and landscaping, our little cottage was full of color and life.

Our sailing magazines piled on the coffee table were soon replaced with books on parenting. I jumped wholeheartedly into my new role, but to maintain our flight benefits and insurance I continued working the night shift at Alaska Airlines. Needless to say, I was a very tired mama.

After feeding Madison and getting her down to sleep, I'd put on my navy polyester uniform, drive blindly through a blizzard, and walk what seemed like a mile to get into the airport. Shivering in my long-oversized parka on the frozen tarmac, I'd greet people from Barrow, Bethel, or Fairbanks bound for places that promised a lei greeting and a mai tai upon arrival.

"What am I doing?" I'd whisper to Paul as I crawled into our warm bed at 4 a.m. Maddi was sprawled out next to her daddy, giving me about a foot of space.

"You, my dear, are getting us out of here," He turned over carefully to avoid waking our baby girl.

Strollers, tools, and toys started filling up our little house. Without a garage, our dwelling suddenly became much smaller. We knew if we wanted another child, we were going to need a bigger home.

One spring evening, we took Madison for a walk in her jogger around Westchester Lagoon. This popular recreational area featured 11 miles of coastal bike path that ran the length of Anchorage.

As we strolled along Wildwood Lane, I saw it first—a for-sale sign stood at the edge of an empty wooded lot, a rare sight in this established neighborhood.

"Wow, this is a great place for a house!" I said, handing Madison her sippy cup. It was the third time she had tossed it out into the street. I glanced at Paul, who was looking at me with a big grin on his face.

Two weeks later our offer was accepted. We were going to build our dream home!

That summer we pored over designs and agreed on a beautiful Cape Cod–style building plan with cedar shingles like those in New England. With the extra hours of summer daylight and grandparents on hand, we finished construction in just under six months. We quickly got to know our friendly neighbors, hosted backyard barbeques, and finally celebrated the fruits of our labor. Just when I thought things couldn't get any better, they did.

Kelsey was born the following spring just as the cherry trees in the front yard bloomed with beautiful pink flowers. With a wisp of blonde hair and big green eyes, we were blessed with another daughter, completing our family perfectly. Quiet and content, Kelsey studied people around her with genuine curiosity. She would play by herself for hours while life buzzed around her. Motherhood was everything I dreamed it would be and so much more; both girls taught me things about myself I never knew existed, and still do. I had found my purpose.

With a three-year age gap, Madison was a huge help to me and entertained her sister while I cooked and cleaned. Paul and I quickly settled into our new home, establishing routines, sharing the chores and baby duties.

Our house was big, comfortable, and full of life. My mom would babysit anytime we wanted a date night. We had a giant playroom filled with every toy imaginable.

But as I wandered throughout the rooms day after day picking up dolls, dishes, and dirty clothes, a nagging question kept rolling around in my head . . .

Is this it?

CHAPTER 7

The Map

Anchorage, Alaska

"You're only one decision away from a totally different life."

—MEL ROBBINS

As the first layer of frost blanketed the grass, the days were getting shorter and to-do lists were getting longer. Our work and home routines were beginning to take a toll on us. Paul had just purchased a 40-unit apartment building in Palmer which included major renovations and time away from the family. While he drove an hour out to the valley every day, I was left to care for the kids. We were optimistic as we planned our future, knowing the income from the apartments would generate enough cash flow for us to spend more time together. That was the goal anyway.

Exhausted after finally getting the girls down for the night, both of us wanted the attention of the other yet were too tired to give it. He renovated buildings, I cleaned up mashed bananas. I didn't have anything to show him but happy and healthy kids. *Was this enough?*

I wanted him to see me as he once did on the bow of our boat—the adventurous girl he married, diving for lobster, dodging reefs and trimming sails. I missed my buddy, my carefree sailor that talked more, laughed louder, and played harder. I missed warm days and sunshine.

As winter approached, the days got colder and darker. Every morning Paul would stop in the playroom for hugs before leaving.

As he showed me his clipboard list of jobs, I was struggling to get skinny jeans on Barbie's long legs.

"This is my day," I said, rolling my eyes.

"We should be out there," he said, pointing to the giant world map on the wall as he walked out the door. "You've got this, honey!" he shouted halfway down the stairs.

Madison had set up a board game, playing Kelsey's pieces for her. "I got to Gumdrop Mountain first!" she shouted with satisfaction.

Kelsey knocked the plastic gingerbread men across the board, grinning. Madison ran off to her bedroom already distracted by something else.

Picking up the game pieces, I glanced up at the big, laminated map tacked on the far side of the room. Paul had brought it home on the last day of his geography class. I had hung it up in the playroom, thinking the girls should be exposed to a world beyond Candyland.

I felt like Gloppy in the molasses swamp . . . stuck.

As I sat on the carpet in a sea of toys, I couldn't help thinking of everywhere else but where I was. I tried to open the windows to breathe in fresh air, but they were frozen shut. I wanted to take the kids for a walk, but it wouldn't be daylight for another three hours. Kelsey discovered her binky on the floor, popped it in her mouth, and was soon mesmerized by Barney, the purple dinosaur on TV.

Tracing a line along the map with my finger, I connected the tiny Pacific Islands down to New Zealand. Sighing, I glanced down at my sweet daughter. She looked up at me, smiling through her pacifier. *I want to give them so much more than this,* I thought, gazing up at the ceiling. I had painted it sky blue with fluffy white clouds. I stared at the forms I made using just a pencil and my imagination, the same color, the same shape, unmoving, every day.

With Kelsey settled into her Boppy pillow, I went to find our three-year-old, who was sitting naked in an empty tub playing with her collection of rubber ducks. She decided when she wanted a bath, and today it was 7 a.m.

I returned to the playroom to pick up the explosion of toys. Sorting the Polly Pockets and Lincoln Logs in their various colorful plastic bins, I realized how much time I spent just cleaning. I scooped up our baby girl.

"Let's go take a bath," I said, smothering her with kisses. She giggled, throwing her head back. As I turned out the light and closed the door, I took one last look at the map.

We gotta get out of here.

CHAPTER 8

Road Trip

Anchorage, Alaska–Fort Lauderdale, Florida

"If we wait until we're ready, we'll be waiting for the rest of our lives."

—LEMONY SNICKET

A laska—Land of the Midnight Sun.

It was another gorgeous summer evening and because the sun didn't set, we often let the girls play long after their usual bedtime. I leaned back in my Adirondack chair on the deck still smelling of fresh varnish.

"How about we *drive* to Florida this year?" I asked Paul, half joking,

We made a point to visit his parents more often since their move to sunny Stuart, Florida.

Swatting a pesky mosquito, I sipped from the bottle of Corona Light Paul had brought out to me. We soaked up these rare moments together. Madison was up in the tree house singing, while Kelsey twirled in her Exersaucer, chewing her way around it.

We agreed our lives needed a shakeup. The more we talked about it, the more real our idea of driving became. *How hard could it be?* An RV is just a home on wheels, but way more adventurous. I thought about Kelsey and how she would do on the road. I looked at our baby, so happy sitting and playing in her new bouncy seat. *That will come too*, I thought, already planning the packing list.

By the time we had tucked the girls into bed that night, we had organized a cross-country road trip that would take us through Canada via the Alaska Highway, across the Midwest and up through New England before heading down the coast to Florida. We would leave in two months to see the leaves change into their golden fall colors.

The following day, Paul was already scouring the internet for motorhomes, while I ordered a new *Milepost* guidebook to begin researching places to visit. My brain was firing on all cylinders again. I felt my batteries recharging as I scrolled through the pages of National Parks, Yogi Bear campgrounds and exciting attractions. We were going on a family adventure!

The hardest part was sharing the news with my parents. I'll never forget the look on my mom's face.

"Isn't Kelsey a little young for such a trip?" she asked, forcing a smile.

As unconventional as it was, I knew our six-month-old would be fine as long as she had her favorite stuffed dog, "Puzzles", her cozy blankie, a portable crib, and her sister.

That August, Paul hired and trained a property manager and bought a used Class A 38-foot Dutch Star motorhome from a retired couple in Girdwood, Alaska. Madison and I carefully chose the best toys and books for the long 5,000-mile journey. It was a little hard leaving the comforts of home, but I would finally close the door on messy rooms and open one that promised new experiences, uninterrupted time with each other, and many lasting memories.

Our rolling home took us through expansive farmland, majestic forests, breathtaking mountain ranges, scenic coastlines, sand dunes, and bustling cities. We visited relatives and friends across the Midwest and stopped in Paul's hometown of Fishkill. We paddled our way through the Great Lakes, hiked the Appalachian trail across the Blue Ridge Mountains, picked roadside pumpkins in Vermont, and ate fresh lobster in Maine.

The devastating news of 9/11 forced us to take a detour to Liberty State Park in Jersey City rather than New York City as originally planned. Looking across the harbor from our campsite, we could still see the smoke and debris.

After putting the girls to bed that night, I joined my husband around the campfire. We both sat staring at the flames, unable to make any sense of the events that took place so close to our family. *God, how are we to raise our girls in such a broken world?* I prayed, thinking of those who woke up that morning kissing their loved ones goodbye. Little did they know it would be their last time.

The fragility of life reinforced our conviction that we were making good decisions for our family. Our hope as parents was to provide our daughters with all they needed to adapt to an ever-changing world with compassion, courage, and resilience.

Back inside our motorhome, we tiptoed past Madison, sound asleep on the pull-out sofa. I stared at our little angel longer than usual, giving her a kiss on the forehead. For a toddler, she embraced life on the road better than we could have imagined. With just a few Beanie Babies and a well-used drawing pad, she entertained herself with an endless imagination. Kelsey simply enjoyed the world around her with innocent, baby curiosity. As soon as we set up the playpen, she would grab Puzzles and fall fast asleep.

I looked forward to every new day but was challenged in ways I never imagined. Paul did all the driving, while I was busy in back with the kids, trying desperately to remain upright. We'd make frequent stops at every historical marker, plaque, monument, or lookout any chance we could get. We had no schedule and took all the time we wanted. While the girls napped, I researched, called, and reserved campgrounds to avoid having to overnight in Walmart parking lots—which wasn't always the worst thing. It had McDonald's, fresh clothes, and a flushing toilet.

After two adventurous months on the road, we finally arrived in Florida enjoying another week with the grandparents.

While there, we sold the motorhome and our tow car getting back what we put into it and so much more. We would soon be returning home with a multitude of memories and stories to share.

Days later, we landed on a snowy airstrip in Anchorage. We were back. Another dark winter lay ahead. There was just one problem.

We couldn't quite figure out how to live in our house again.

CHAPTER 9

What If

Stuart, Florida

"One life. Just one.
Why aren't we running like we are on fire towards our wildest dreams?"

—DEEP TRIVEDI

Upon our return to Alaska, *Cruising World* and *Sailing* magazines started mysteriously appearing on our coffee table again. I thought Paul's subscription had ended.

"How about that?" he'd say, pointing to the glossy cover as he flopped into the corner of our new sectional. It was a picture of a sailboat anchored in clear aquamarine water. Sunbathers in colorful swimwear lounged on the deck, while others snorkeled nearby. Paul looked at me with a weary smile. It was his third attempt at putting "Pip" and "Squeak" to bed—his nicknames for the girls.

Staring out at our backyard now covered in snow, we were both feeling the grip of winter staleness again. It had only been a few months since the road trip, and even as we settled back into our work routines, we were already thinking of where to go next.

One morning, as I wiped a melted popsicle from the table, I paused to stare at the magazine cover. I could almost feel the colors – warm, inviting, adventurous. I sighed, looking out through the icicle-framed sliding glass doors. The treehouse sat frosted over and empty. As a child, I didn't mind the winters. Building snowmen, sledding, and skating were loads of fun. Winter was just another season . . . it was all I knew.

As an adult, I simply didn't want to repeat the life I had all over again with our own children. I didn't just want to "get through" the long cold months. I wanted to run and play outside with our girls, without the daily struggle of endless snow gear, winter colds, and waiting for the sun to shine again.

Our intentions to own a home were good. It seemed like the normal thing to do. Raise kids, put them in school, sports, and music classes and eventually send them off to college. As big and beautiful as our house was, it didn't seem to bring us more joy, just a lot of stress and separation. My brother and sisters had all moved away to warmer climates to raise their own families. And despite our good friends and my parents living nearby, I often felt a bit isolated and alone.

I looked around. My mind was as cluttered as the living room. Paul and I didn't come right out and say it at first, but I knew we both felt it. The years spent talking about how we wanted to structure our lives, grow our wealth, live simply, and travel. What happened to that? How were we supposed to do that with kids, a new house, and responsibilities?

Spending Christmas break with the Florida in-laws proved a good remedy for our winter blues as well as a respite from all these nagging questions. While "Nana and Pappy" babysat the girls for date night, Paul and I drove to Conchy Joe's Bar and Grill along Jensen Beach. It had become our favorite waterfront hangout whenever we were in Stuart.

Old sailors' T-shirts and boat flags hung from the thatched roof above our heads. A familiar reggae song played from a nearby jukebox.

"I love this," I said to Paul licking the salt-encrusted rim of my glass. The warm air, heavy with humidity, reminded me of our early days at sea. Paul was unusually relaxed as we watched boat after boat come in at sunset. For two uninterrupted hours, we talked about life, our future and laughed more than we had in a long time. As I went to dip a tortilla chip in salsa, Paul reached across the table taking my hand in his.

"Honey, what if we just sold everything?" he asked, suddenly more serious. "What if we just buy a boat and sail away?" His words sounded crazy. The good kind of crazy.

I chuckled nervously, glancing around to see who might be listening. The Bahamian inspired restaurant was packed, yet I felt like we were the only two in the room.

Paul continued holding my hand as intently as he held my gaze. He wasn't joking this time.

I looked away as tears welled up in my eyes. I removed my sunglasses and saw he was tearing up, too. I knew at that very moment this was the beginning of something big, an unspoken dream both of us had been keeping inside yet too afraid to share.

It just took a couple margaritas and a little Bob Marley to finally get it out.

CHAPTER 10

Boat Hunting

"She may not be the most popular or prettiest but if you love her and she makes you smile what else matters?"

−BOB MARLEY

When he wasn't snowplowing or thawing frozen pipes, Paul was once again searching the internet—this time looking for the perfect boat, our next home. While the girls played quietly, I would flip to the back of *Cruising World* magazines, studying all the different makes and models of sailboats. Choosing the right one, suitable for offshore cruising, was more difficult than I had thought.

"These are good problems to have!" Paul reminded me when I got overwhelmed with choices. Recalling a catamaran he had seen years before when we owned *Scarlett*, we revised our search to include two hulls rather than one. Space and stability with small children on board seemed the logical choice.

In the spring, our family flew to Anacortes, Washington, to check out a listed catamaran as well as explore the beautiful San Juan Islands. We had no intention of buying such a new boat, but the owner was generous enough to arrange a tour.

As we walked to the end of the dock, the 47-foot boat came into view. I had never seen anything like it in my life. It was so wide and intimidating, with every feature one could imagine.

I watched closely as Madison jumped on the bow's large trampolines. "I didn't know boats had these!" she shouted, bouncing her baby sister across the netting. After a walk-through of the entire vessel, I was sold on the spacious cabins, huge galley, and sunlight-filled salon.

The broker had been washing one side of the boat. "Wanna turn it around? I need to scrub the other side anyway!"

Without hesitation, Paul took the helm. After a quick rundown, he was circling back and out, pulling it effortlessly alongside the dock where the girls and I stood with our mouths open.

"Like a glove!" he said impersonating Jim Carrey from *Ace Ventura: Pet Detective.*

After exchanging business cards, we returned to our little beach house rental on Orcas Island. While the girls collected sea glass and shells, Paul and I walked along the shore discussing our recent experience. We both agreed we'd start looking for a catamaran in Florida, but more within our budget.

After many months of searching, an ad in *Multihull* magazine caught Paul's attention. The owner had just sailed from England to West Palm Beach, Florida, and was ready to pass his boat on to someone else ready to start their own adventure. The 50-foot, custom-built catamaran was fully equipped for offshore sailing.

Paul flew down to meet the owner and emailed me a video of the entire boat. Although it needed many upgrades it came with a nice price tag and many comfortable features we were looking for. Paul convinced me that fixing her up would be part of the journey and we'd get to know the boat very intimately.

After a lengthy sea-trial, Paul's offer was accepted. He remained in Stuart, Florida, living with his parents while getting the major upgrades underway. These included waxing the hulls, a new watermaker and upgrading the navigational equipment.

Back home, I had the daunting responsibility of sharing the big news with Maddi and Kelsey. Since our trip to the San Juans, they seemed happy about our "live aboard" idea, but children have short memories - perhaps they had changed their minds. It was easy to talk about when on vacation, but the thrill can be lost when one returns to the familiar routines and comforts of home. To kids, selling everything to go live on a boat could either be the most exciting adventure or their worst nightmare. I had to choose my words and timing carefully.

I found them together one day coloring quietly in the playroom.

"Girls come over here for a minute, I have something exciting to tell you!" I said, sitting crisscross in the middle of the room. I opened my arms as they ran over and dove into my lap.

"You know how Daddy is in Florida looking at boats for us, right?"

"Yep, did he find one?" Maddi looked up at me hopefully with her big brown eyes.

"Yes! He finally found us a sailboat! It's a catamaran like the one we saw in Washington, remember? With the big trampolines?"

"I loved that boat, it was so fun!" she laughed, tickling her little sister. At just a year old, Kelsey didn't understand quite what was going on. She simply noticed when Madison was happy, and that was enough for her.

I carefully explained the process of moving onboard, meeting new friends, and all the amazing places we would visit.

Madison jumped up and started dancing around the room. Her brown hair was cut in a short straight bob like the cartoon character, Dora the Explorer. It swished back and forth as she looked around at all the toys as if already planning what she would take along.

"Can Beary come?" she asked, grabbing her big stuffed bear from the floor, giving him a squishy hug.

"Of course, we can't leave Beary!" I laughed, breathing a sigh of relief.

And then came the dreaded question, "What about our house?"

I explained that it would now be passed on to another family with children, giving them a chance to enjoy a house with a big playroom. I promised we'd keep our most special things in storage. After a long pause she nodded, content with the plan.

While Paul continued boat improvements in Florida, I began planning and packing. First, I bought a three-ring binder with several dividers and labels to organize our mammoth-sized move. Next, I researched all vaccinations needed to enter certain countries and updated our passports. Like a scavenger hunt, I ticked off must-have items and made a blueprint for where to store it all. School supplies, foul weather gear and all-season clothing, birthday gifts, various holiday and crafts supplies, toiletries, gifts to pass out, long-life food items, toys, DVDs, and medical supplies. The lists went on and on.

I had the girls draw boats, read about boats, make boat crafts, and sing songs about boats. Telling them about our plan was one thing, holding onto the momentum was another. By sharing the activities they felt like an important part of the crew – which they were!

I ordered the accredited homeschool Calvert curriculum for pre-K and 2nd grade. It was like Christmas when their boxes arrived on our doorstep! New textbooks, pencils, paints, workbooks, and even T-shirts emblazoned with the Calvert School logo would come along with us for their first year of "boat school."

We donated most of their toys to charity, researched countries we'd visit, and read about how other families lived on boats. We found creative ways to make the move just as memorable as the event. The road trip a year earlier helped tremendously. Living in an RV for eight weeks gave us a trial run traveling together in a small space.

The girls seemed just as excited about this dream of ours even when I was quite anxious myself. I spent many sleepless nights roaming the house, wondering if our plan was absolutely crazy. I knew in my heart we had to do this. I was certain that there was so much more for Paul and me to experience together as parents and a narrow window of time for us to cherish our daughters' childhood years. I didn't want to miss a single moment.

Our date nights now included studying sailing routes and taping up boxes bound for our long-term storage unit. Some items like our baby's first footprints, photos, books, and files were irreplaceable and needed a forever home. We made one final family trip to West Palm Beach to put the finishing touches on the boat. While Paul was ordering new charts and spare parts I had the cockpit cushions reupholstered in red Sunbrella fabric and sewed colorful pillows and curtains to match.

In between sanding and painting the hulls, we would take the girls to nearby parks, gardens, and museums. The secret was to balance chores with fun excursions and before long, they never knew the difference!

While a new cockpit cork floor was being installed, the original worn trampoline was replaced with a new nylon net. With as much bouncing as our kids would do, it needed to be safe and strong. We gathered medicines, syringes, stitch kits, braces, bandages, splints, a blood pressure cuff, ear drops, eyewash, antibiotics, a stethoscope, and even a defibrillator for our large orange first aid kit.

Kelsey and Madison's cabin bunks were decorated with tropical fish bedding, colorful pictures, and hammocks to store their belongings. They were allowed ten or so toys each, with a shared bookshelf that held all the best classics they had chosen for the journey. Favorite stuffed animals were selected carefully, as the drag-along companions would provide security and comfort during long passages and stormy nights. Simply moving aboard was a grand adventure; the more we packed the more exciting it all became.

After six very busy months, we were finally ready.

All we needed now was a name.

CHAPTER 11

Ohana

"Ohana means family.
Family means no one gets left behind or forgotten."

—LILO AND STITCH

My dad's old fishing boat, the *Damnifiknow*, still sits on a trailer in the backyard where I grew up. As a child, I'd stare at it from my bedroom window—a comforting sight decorated with a tangled collection of plastic duck decoys and dip nets. An old, chipped Mercury motor precariously hangs off the back.

What should our boat's name say about us? I wondered.

We agreed it should be easy to say over the handheld radio and represent who we are as a family. Having been owned by a Dutch tulip farmer, the word "Tulipa" was painted along the sides with a colorful orange tulip. Although it was considered bad luck to change a boat's name, we knew it needed to be done.

Night after night, Paul searched the internet.

"How about *Freedom, Island Time, Seas the Day*?" he would ask me, going down the list. Nothing stuck. We decided to give it a rest. The name would find us.

One afternoon, I took the girls to see the Disney animated movie, *Lilo and Stitch*. The story is about a little blue Koala-like creature created by genetic experimentation on another planet. "Stitch" escapes to Earth landing in Hawaii where he impersonates a dog and gets adopted by Lilo, a little island girl. Over time, Stitch does a little soul-searching and begins to understand the meaning of love and family.

During a particular moment in the movie, Stitch says, "*Ohana* means family. Family means no one gets left behind or forgotten."

At that moment, Madison leaned over her little sister and whispered to me, "Mommy! That's what we should name our boat—*Ohana!*"

It was the perfect name.

CHAPTER 12

The Right Thing

"Twenty years from now you will be more disappointed by the things you didn't do than by the ones you did do. So throw off the bowlines. Sail away from the safe harbor. Catch the trade winds in your sails. Explore. Dream. Discover."

—MARK TWAIN

House for sale.

The sign in our front yard might as well have said, "No going back now." I found it fascinating how a single decision can change a life so quickly.

We put Madison in a half-day summer Montessori program to keep her busy while I continued packing and planning. As Kelsey and I waved goodbye to her from the school gate, our little girl ran over to her new friends for hugs. This part was the hardest.

What are we doing? I anxiously thought to myself, strapping Kelsey into her car seat. As we drove away my eyes welled up with tears. I looked in the rearview mirror. Our one-year-old was humming a *VeggieTales* song while munching on her goldfish crackers. She looked back at me with a big grin on her face. I smiled back, quickly wiping my eyes.

Pacing the house at night, I'd peek into Maddi's bedroom. She looked so peaceful sleeping under the sailboat quilt Nana made for her. I would make sure it came with us—familiar items would provide security and a piece of home. Her artwork was tacked on a bulletin board above her little yellow desk. She and I had painted colorful flower stencils on every wall. As I continued wandering down the hallway, I bent down and picked up Kelsey's binky. She had several positioned all over the house, unwilling to give them up. Carefully opening her door, I was greeted with the fresh, clean smell of baby powder. Our sweet girl rolled over, hugging Sunny, a stuffed orange reindeer she took everywhere. How would they adapt to life at sea? I wondered. How can we take them away from all this?

As I gently closed her door, I turned and tripped on the thick rug, a recent purchase from Pottery Barn. I shook my head, thinking of all the time and energy I put into choosing it; the hours and days picking out paint colors to perfectly coordinate with our new furnishings, only to sell it all.

Not everyone was going to like our plan. We finally broke the news to my parents. Unable to tell them when or *if* we'd be back, I could almost feel my mom's heart breaking. She had so much love for her grandchildren and would miss them terribly. I knew our leaving would now top her list of worries, but just as they left Minnesota and their families to live out their own dream, this was ours. I hated this part the most, but we'd try and return for Christmases and invited them to stay with us on *Ohana*. Our friends had mixed feelings. Most were thrilled for us, while others shook their heads and said, "Just wait, you'll be back."

This was not a vacation, however. This was not a phase. Leaving was something we felt necessary – for us, for our family. Right or wrong, we had to find out for ourselves.

Our house only had to be shown once. As predicted, it was sold to a lovely couple with children. Handing the keys over was a bittersweet but exciting exchange—one lifestyle for another.

What took months to build took a week to undo.

I was equal parts melancholy, overwhelmed and incredibly excited all at the same time.

There were so many emotions and tears shed that summer, but I knew there was no going back. Although I loved the little neighborhood life we created, I felt more alive than I ever thought possible.

Overall, it took us three months to train property managers, upgrade and provision *Ohana*, and get her seaworthy. Finally, after a wide-eyed Alaska Airlines agent checked our eight heavy duffel bags, two strollers and four passports, we were on a plane bound for West Palm Beach, Florida. Our new floating home was waiting for us.

Soon we were joined by grandparents, aunts, uncles, and cousins who made a special trip to see us off. After a dockside dinner, they lined up along the pier to bid us farewell. I felt like I should be waving a hand-kerchief like back in the old-time ocean liner days. I remember the tears my mom tried to hide behind her big sunglasses as she hugged Madison and Kelsey tightly.

It was one of the most difficult moments of my life. Paul's parents gave us confident, back-patting hugs as if they knew this had been their son's plan since he was a little boy. My sister's husband, a boat captain himself, tossed us the last of our lines. "You're living the dream, Bergers." he said as his blue eyes welled up with tears.

As we slowly motored away, our people in the distance grew smaller. The arm-waving soon became hands on the hips followed by a slow saunter up the ramp. And then they were gone.

Madison and Kelsey bounced on the trampolines, already making up games to play. Watching them carefully, I stowed the fenders in the foredeck lockers while Paul drove us out. We were sailing away, and these two little humans relied on and trusted us completely. We would not let them down. I felt an overwhelming responsibility, different from when we were safe in our land home. My rational side craved order, logic, and good sense. This had none of those things.

A rush of adrenaline surged through my body. Everything I had learned from my life experiences thus far had led me to this moment. Paul and I had equipped ourselves to survive and thrive out here. I felt fully convinced that we were making a difference for our family, trusting God, and following the direction of our dreams.

With our daughters' tiny hands wrapped around our fingers, we looked out at our new water world from the bow. As we rounded the sea wall, the expansive ocean took my breath away . . . blue for as far as the eye could see.

Here we go.

I closed my eyes and exhaled. Our new life lay ahead just beyond the horizon. We had it all—a boat, time, and each other.

This was the right thing.

SECTION 2

Fire

CHAPTER 13

Comfort Zone

Nassau, Bahamas

*"One of the greatest discoveries a man makes, one of his great surprises,
is to find he can do what he was afraid he couldn't do."*

—HENRY FORD

A sticky note on my college bathroom mirror read, "FEAR: Forget Everything and Run or Face Everything and Rise."

So, when Paul asked me to scale our 63-foot mast to change out the anchor light before sailing south to the Exumas, I pulled out that little nugget of wisdom.

I'm not a fan of heights, but I was the obvious choice—strong, flexible, and light enough for Paul to winch up. I looked up at the top, thinking how far away it was, and then at Madison, who had already scrambled across the boom and into our red canvas sail cover.

"Hi Mom!" she said, waving proudly.

"Okay, let's do this!" I clapped my hands. I wasn't about to wimp out in front of my girls. With the boat tied securely along the dock, Paul gave me very specific instructions as he reached into the cockpit storage locker. The small bosun chair was basically a black rubber seat like those toddler playground swings with two leg holes.

"Really?" I said with a raised eyebrow. Paul just laughed and clipped a carabiner from the seat to a line he had rigged onto a winch.

"You'll be fine!" he assured me, tightening the harness. I loved his confidence in me.

For a second, as I slid my bare legs through, I felt like Sarah Connor in the movie, *The Terminator*. I asked myself, *what would she do?* I just needed a pair of aviators.

Showing me the new LED light bulb, Paul explained the process very carefully.

"Got it!" I said, distracted by Kelsey, who had toddled out with green stuff all over her face. Turning my chin back to meet his eyes, he had me confirm his directions.

"Just don't drop it," Paul said tucking the little bulb into a pocket on the seat. "You've got this!" he yelled after returning to the cockpit. No sooner had he started cranking me up, than the swinging began.

"Wrap your legs around the mast! Then pull out the footholds and step on them as you climb!" he yelled, giving me a thumbs-up.

Like a spider monkey, I gripped the smooth white mast and started the ascent. Kelsey and Madison were now sitting on the top deck to watch the show.

"Go, Mama!" They clapped and waved at me as I climbed higher. Kelsey was nibbling on a sugar cookie. *Ahh yes, the green frosting,* I remembered. It was St. Patrick's Day, and we never missed a holiday, even at sea.

Seeing their sweet, smiling faces made me feel like a superhero. If only I had a cape! Once I got past the last foothold, my legs took over. Like a contestant on *American Ninja Warrior,* I scrambled up the pole that started to thin out as I climbed, my body wrapping around it more tightly, like a pretzel. I felt a sudden chill. *Oh, my gosh, is that a cloud? Am I in a cloud?* My heart started pounding. Knowing I might panic if I looked away from the mast, I took a deep breath to calm down. I spied a passing seagull out of the corner of my eye and caught a glimpse of the harbor, the bridge to Paradise Island where I ran each day, and the boats at anchor. What an awesome perspective it was! I felt so alive! This time last year, I was sitting in my minivan, crying in a Home Depot parking lot. Today I was clinging to a mast on our sailboat with my family cheering me on. My view had clearly changed.

At that moment, a strong gust of wind shook the boat a little. Snapping back to reality, I gave Paul a motion to continue winching me up. I carefully scaled the last three feet without looking down and got to work. I didn't want to be up here when the wind picked up again. I carefully removed the bulb from the side pocket as if it were a holy relic.

I removed the cover, twisted out the old light and retrieved the new one from the side pocket. Screwing it carefully into place, I replaced the cover, closed my eyes, and finally exhaled. I did it.

I yelled to Paul that I was ready to come down. He double wrapped the line around the drum and started cranking.

63 feet, 53, 43, 30, 10 . . . my toes finally connected with the deck. Madison and Kelsey helped me out of my harness, hugging my legs. My sweaty husband gave me a congratulatory fist pump before going below to flip the switch on the electrical panel.

"Is it on?" he yelled up.

"*Yes,* it is!" I called back, relieved. He met me at the bow, putting an arm around me. "Good job, honey!"

I looked up at our new light with pride. I had done something I didn't want to do, something I was afraid to do.

Nelson Mandela once said, "the brave man is not he who does not feel afraid, but he who conquers that fear.

I couldn't agree more.

CHAPTER 14

Shell Yeah!

Georgetown, Great Exuma, Bahamas

"We were never meant to live life accumulating stuff.
We were meant to live simply enjoying the experiences of life,
the people of life, and the journey of life—not the things of life."

—JOSHUA BECKER

Paul had no sooner tied our inflatable dinghy to the old wooden dock when the girls bounced from its rubber sides, their little bare feet hitting the sand. Off they ran into the casuarina trees as if they were on a Navy SEALs mission.

We had found a perfect place to anchor *Ohana,* about 40 yards from the shoreline. Once I secured the bridle on the anchor rode to prevent us from swinging, I noticed several pink conch shells in the shallows. *I am definitely diving for those later,* I thought as I inspected my lines.

We dropped our hook in front of the monohulls anchored out on Stocking Island in the Exuma Cays. Having a 3 ½ foot shallow draft gave us an advantage. Even our toddler could swim to shore safely. More boats would arrive before sundown. Like little hobbits emerging from their holes, kids would appear from below decks while their parents motored around, looking for the ideal spot. Wives would yell at their husbands, unable to make out anchoring hand signals. Barking dogs would scurry around the decks while naked children, one of whom had just made eye contact with Kelsey, tripped their way to the bow.

"They have kids! Look, there's two girls on that boat!" A little boy from the next boat cried out.

Once anchors were deployed, all inhabitants would dive overboard as if it were the start of an ocean swim race. Using any form of floatation device they could find, bodies of all shapes and sizes would make their way to the shore. The colorful flotilla of foam noodles, kayaks, kickboards, and dinghies was a sight to behold. Tanned bodies would drip dry their way to the outdoor tiki bar with plastic storage bags of cash strapped haphazardly around their waist or tucked in a bikini top.

After setting up the homemade cupcakes and gifts on a weathered yellow picnic table, Paul and I welcomed our friends, who had joined us on Hamburger Beach for Kelsey's second birthday party. From behind their drink coolers, umbrellas, and snorkel gear emerged five more children covered head to toe in blue zinc sunscreen.

Boat kids make quick friends. They don't even bother to look each other over. They know they're small and stuck on a boat by force. Instantly bonded by this mutual understanding, the alliance between these young sailors is refreshing and instant. They'd run off together with a tribal-like energy to explore their new island playground. Our rule was that they simply stay within earshot. If our girls couldn't hear us calling, they had gone too far. Off they'd scramble to climb trees or play tag while Paul and I met up with new friends at the famous Chat 'N' Chill bar and grill on the beach. This laid-back, barefoot beach bar is the quintessential cruiser's hangout. With island music blaring from the outdoor speakers, sailors from all over the world would gather for hamburgers and a well-deserved ice-cold Kalik beer.

The islands of The Bahamas were a perfect place to begin our journey and introduce our little crew to their new lifestyle. Just 50 miles off the coast of Florida, the 700 breathtaking islands are surrounded by white sand beaches and shallow crystalline waters teeming with colorful fish and coral. Maddi and Kelsey slept soundly during our first night-crossing from Dinner Key, Florida, waking up in a tropical paradise.

The Bahamas were far enough that we could experience our first night offshore together as a family, yet close enough to sail back as soon as our new bimini top, main sail, and upholstered cushions were finished. This shakedown cruise was a great way to get our feet wet.

Our birthday girl was already zigzagging up and down the shore chasing after sand crabs.

Meanwhile, Madison had rounded up all the boat kids and organized an event—a self-imposed responsibility she took very seriously.

"Mom! Mom! Mommy!" she yelled breathlessly, returning with her shirt full of tiny snail shells. "We're playing a birthday game! We are seeing how many we can find and whatever team has the most wins!" she explained, shaking with excitement.

"Okay, I have a container here, and maybe grab that old box over there for the other kids," I said, pointing to a pile of recycled bottles behind a pink stucco hut that said "Women." *Good to know,* I thought. Toilets are rare out here on the islands. If there wasn't one, it meant finding a bush or going for a swim.

After a full day of beach volleyball, tree swinging and collecting sand dollars, it was time to head back to *Ohana.* I packed up Kelsey's homemade birthday gifts and remnants of cupcakes now frosted with sand flies. The parents called their kids back to the dinghies, some catching a ride with new pals. Our girls returned smiling and sweaty from their all-day treasure hunt. Their skinny arms held out their overflowing plastic ice-cream containers loaded with shells. There must have been over a hundred.

"Look at how many we found!" Madison said boosting Kelsey into the boat. "We're going to make necklaces for all our friends!"

I collected the dinghy anchor while Paul pushed us off the sand into deeper water.

Back onboard, the girls and I poured the gray shells into several plastic sandwich bags for safekeeping and found a secure place for them in the craft drawers. Cozying up in our own bunk after settling the kids in for the night, I read a couple of chapters from my Michael Crichton novel before finally closing my eyes. Wearing contact lenses out here made my eyes sting, so I was often ready to shut them right after the girls went down about 9 p.m. Paul was already fast asleep, wedged against the bulkhead, avoiding my reading light. Clicking it off, I soon dozed as well, lulled to sleep by the clinking of a loose halyard against the mast like a wind chime.

Two hours later I bolted upright, awakened by something that sounded like the sharp claws on a cat trapped in a closet. Since living on a boat, my sense of hearing became my superpower. This was a strange new sound—close, near my head. I pressed an ear against the fiberglass wall that separated us from the ocean world, the scratching and scuffling growing louder. I turned on my flashlight that I kept on a small shelf next to our bunk. All became quiet again. *Maybe just barnacles*, I thought as I turned off the light and lay back down. *Scritch, scratch, tap, tap.* I couldn't take it anymore.

"Honey, wake up!" I finally shook Paul out of his coma.

We searched everywhere in the darkness, stopping to listen, checking where the sounds were coming from. It was common to hear crackling and popping under our boat as there was an entire ecosystem down there that thrived on anything that attached itself to our hulls.

I rested my head against the sliding door of our cabin. I never closed it fully as I wanted to hear the girls should they call out at night. They loved having "their side of the boat" to themselves although I still felt that they were too far away.

As the noises grew louder, I slid our door slowly to one side. I was shocked to find not one but more than 30 hermit crabs creeping their way along the bottom edge of the track. Like little marching crustacean soldiers, their open claws grasped for a grip on anything while tediously dragging their shells behind them.

"Ewwwwww!!!" I shrieked looking around for anything I could brush them into. I grabbed a straw basket hanging from a hook. Paul and I frantically started sweeping them into it while following the trail to the others. We instantly knew where they had come from—the girls' shell collection!

We spent the rest of the night rounding up all the hermit crabs that had clawed their way out of the plastic baggies. Carrying their homes on their backs, they had managed to make the long journey through the drawer and into every crack and crevice on the boat. We sealed them all in a big plastic container until we could release them back onto the beach the following day.

We returned to our bunk, laughing. "I can't wait to tell the kids in the morning!" I said as we crawled back in. Unable to sleep from all the excitement, I stared out the open ceiling hatch above my head. A cool breeze made its way in, soothing my sunburned skin.

I thought about our life now, how simple, and stress-free it was.

A year ago, we were arguing over what kind of sofa to buy. A year ago, I was bawling in a sea of Legos. A year ago, we sat in a home that was just too big for us.

Like the hermit crabs outgrowing their shells, we found a new one as well.

It was the perfect fit.

CHAPTER 15

Triathlons and Tequila

Puerto Aventuras, Quintana Roo, Mexico

"If it doesn't challenge you, it doesn't change you."

—FRED DEVITO

With a golf course, quaint shops, restaurants, world-class resorts, and the largest dolphin habitat in the Yucatan Peninsula, the boating community of Puerto Aventuras became our home base for the next year.

We hadn't planned to stay that long, but the whole idea behind our family slowing down was to do just that . . . slow down. If we liked a place and were having fun, we stayed. We also wanted to give Kelsey and Madison enough time to meet some new friends while learning about the Mexican culture.

Because of our preliminary trip to the Bahamas, the girls had gotten their sea legs. This two-day passage out of Key West was a walk in the park. With *Ohana's* 27-foot wide beam we were given a slip along the entrance to the marina with an expansive view of the inlet. Needless to say, the sunsets were out of this world.

Every morning, a parade of catamarans and tour boats would motor out of the harbor for dive excursions, snorkeling, and fishing trips. Our girls would stand at the bow waving to bikini-clad tourists dancing to the music blaring over the boat's speakers.

Just steps down from our pier was the world-famous Dolphin Dreams—a place where people could swim with the playful dolphins and interact with sea lions and manatees. The trainers' high-pitched whistle became our alarm clock every morning. We had to walk past the outdoor pools to get to the marina parking lot, usually during feeding or training time. The girls knew each dolphin by name and said hello to them as if they were old friends. They'd get a waving flipper in return.

After a month of exploring the Riviera Maya, we enrolled Madison and Kelsey in a half-day program at Colegio Puerto Aventuras, a little private school within walking distance from *Ohana*. They needed a bit of structure and social time while learning some Spanish as well. Exchanging their well-worn swimsuits for crisp blue uniform dresses, we watched from the gate as they ran to meet new friends. Paul and I made the most of every adult minute until it was time to retrieve them. We played golf, kayaked, swam in the resort pool, and ate our way through the myriad of amazing restaurants surrounding the marina.

Although I was getting used to the tourist life, we had to get back to reality. Our list of projects was endless, as there was always something to do, fix, or clean on a boat.

We made many acquaintances around the marina that year, and Paul became especially friendly with one guy in particular. Wearing cutoff shorts and old surf T-shirts, Richart Sowa was somewhat of a celebrity around Puerto Aventuras. The charming, long-haired Englishman was considered the eccentric local who wandered the marina barefoot, looking for people to talk to.

Famous for building an eco-friendly island entirely out of plastic bottles, Paul and Richart worked on "Spiral Island" almost daily. They dived under the roots of plants and trees that held the island together by a shroud of netting tying off Sprite and Pepsi containers. After school, the girls and I would kayak out to pet the many cats he kept on the island. I'd find him and Paul sitting in broken lawn chairs together, sipping coconuts while trying to solve the world's problems. This man-made oasis was featured on the Discovery Channel, but sadly Hurricane Emily came and swept the thousands of bottles back into the sea. Richart's intentions were good, but in the end, nature does what it will do.

While Paul continued to busy himself in the engine room or run the family business from a laptop, I would go on my daily "walkabout." Although I loved making new friends around the marina, I valued this time alone. Along Fatima Bay's 1.5-mile stretch of white sand, I discovered an outdoor lap pool and cycle studio at a beachfront resort. Walking through the lobby, I peeked inside only to make eye contact with a very athletic instructor who was barking out commands to a group of sweaty cyclists. He waved me inside using the universal gesture to get on a bike, pointing to one in the front row. Happy I put on shorts that day, I spent the next hour spinning and trying to figure out what "Abajo!" and "Ariba!" meant. It didn't take long to get the idea. Motivated for any new activity besides kayaking and yoga, I bought a 30-day pass and spent the next few weeks finding my leg muscles again.

Showing steady improvement, Rodrigo encouraged me to register for the upcoming Cancun Triathlon—an internationally recognized event that drew participants from all over the world. Although completely out of my comfort zone, the Olympic distance triathlon would be something worthwhile to train for while the kids completed their semester of school.

Once the girls were dropped off and settled into their classrooms, Paul and I went our separate ways, meeting up two hours later for lunch at Gringo Dave's Cantina. I'd run to the studio, cycle for an hour, swim a mile in the outdoor pool, and dry off in a lounge chair in the hot Caribbean sun. I remember thinking, *I never want this to end.*

After two months of this routine, I was ready for the big race. Using all the Spanish terms I had learned in a little class offered in the back of a grocery store, I rented a beautiful Specialized racing bike in the city. While in Cancun, we treated ourselves to a first-class resort experience, complete with a water park and all-you-can-eat buffets.

For the event, we booked a room in a quaint boutique hotel near the start of the race. At the crack of dawn, my family helped me set up my bike, towel, and running shoes in a neat pile in my designated spot amongst rows of high-tech road bikes. I had participated in a couple of small triathlons back home in Anchorage, but this was next-level competition. At the edge of the shoreline, shivering with hundreds of Lycra-clad athletes, I looked back at my family before putting on my goggles. *Show them what Mama can do!* I thought as I dove into the pounding surf.

I don't know what it was that day, maybe it was all my training, the belief I had in myself to do this very hard thing, or that my children would be watching me cross the finish line, but I felt like a champion already. I had never biked 40 kilometers that fast in my life. I had never swam in the open ocean with thrashing bodies crawling over me, nor run 10 kilometers in 90-degree heat. And I had never felt happier as I fell into my family's arms with a race medal around my neck.

Traveling with small children requires tremendous energy, strength, courage, and stamina. By training for this event early on, I had conditioned myself for many strenuous and physical situations on land and sea. From heavy-weather sail handling, fighting off wild dogs with two kids on my back, or rowing against a four-knot current in a storm, I would be physically prepared for these and many unforeseen events during our travels.

After the race, we packed up our rental car and celebrated over dinner at the popular Señor Frog's restaurant with the other competitors. The servers plopped giant sombreros on our heads as we sang along with the live mariachi band.

The following day we visited the archaeological site of Chichén Itzá. Because it was too steep, I stayed behind with Kelsey while Paul and Madison joined others climbing the 182 steps with the help of a line anchored down the middle. Once at the top, they waved to us and then disappeared. My heart was in my stomach. It was terrifying to see our five-year-old that high without any barricade to stop her from falling. *Please hold her hand Paul, please hold her hand.* I kept repeating to myself.

When it came to raising kids, I was more of the protector, always researching and working out scenarios anticipating things that could go wrong. Although it was difficult for me to let go, I wanted our kids to experience life, learning from a "warrior mother", not a "worrier mother." I put my faith in God, trusted my husband and let the girls find their wings.

They soon reappeared from the dark temple rooms they had been exploring. "Hi, guys!" Madison shouted down to us from the 98-foot-tall pyramid. I could finally breathe again.

It was our role to teach our daughters to be brave and jump into new things, encouraging them to fail, get back up, and climb to the top.

Like my triathlon, there were a number of reasons to be fearful, but a million ways to fly as well.

And fly they did.

CHAPTER 16

Moonshadow

Isla Mujeres, Mexico

"Oh, I'm bein' followed by a moonshadow,
moonshadow, moonshadow."

—CAT STEVENS

We called it the "Captain Ron" boat.

The old double-ended ketch was adorned with so many objects that we couldn't imagine anyone actually living onboard. We had met the crew of *Moonshadow* five months earlier in Isla Mujeres, Mexico. The girls were surprised and delighted when they saw two young girls emerge from below, scrambling their way to the bow. I'm not sure if they were screaming or singing.

"There are girls on that boat!" Maddi ran to the nav station to hail them on the radio. Before she could switch channels, sailor banter had begun, and a beach gathering was already organized for all the new arrivals.

After throwing my hair into a couple of salt-stiff braids, I made a batch of my famous corn fritters and honey butter. It's an unspoken rule that cruisers bring a beverage or appetizer to share, and this was my go-to contribution. With the lack of ingredients on most islands, one had to get creative in the galley. Amazing what Bisquick, Wesson oil, and canned corn can produce!

Dinghies of all shapes and sizes would swerve their way onto the beach, their inhabitants waving politely as they passed. Our girls' biggest joy was to hold the tiller and drive our inflatable to shore. While Kelsey showed off her steering skills, Paul would cut the engine before some unlucky swimmer met their demise.

Once we set our anchor firmly in the sand, we were enthusiastically greeted by a short woman in a sarong and a threadbare bikini top. With her long mop of bleached blonde curls, Sheira was a sight to behold.

Her husband Howard loped behind her. A behemoth of a man, this large New Zealander grinned a gap-tooth smile, hollering, "G'day, mate!" to everyone on shore.

The two girls we had seen earlier on the boat belonged to this quirky couple and soon our free-range kids ran down the beach in search of other small boat-dwellers for a game of tug of war.

Who would guess that our initial meeting with this family from down under would share so many future adventures and become such a special part of our sailing story? Honestly, I have no idea how they managed to sail anywhere. *Moonshadow* was so overloaded with possessions that it was hard to make out any cockpit or see any topsides resembling a deck, let alone a steering wheel. Sarongs decorated with the moon and stars clung to the shrouds with clothespins serving as shade canopies around the entire perimeter, blocking out every inch of sunshine. Nevertheless, this eccentric family grew on us, and we became fast friends.

While Sheira's blue eyes grew bigger with every hilarious story she told, her 12-year-old daughter, Rachel, was just the opposite—soft-spoken and squinty-eyed, with a long cascade of red hair. No matter how warm the weather, she was often dressed in an elaborate costume casting "spells" with her magic wand.

A smaller version of her mother, eight-year-old Joslyn had a tangled mane of white-blonde curls that jumped up and down as her body shook with excitement. I can't imagine someone with that much energy being cooped up on a sailboat, but whatever was stored up she released once on land. Dressed in pink or purple, Joslyn resembled a mermaid but had the temperament of a Jack Russell Terrier. While our family dined on tacos and fresh ceviche at our favorite cantina, Joslyn would pop out of nowhere, sit down, and eat whatever was on the table. "What's up, guys?" she'd say, grabbing a handful of tortilla chips. Often the sisters would come aboard *Ohana* at the crack of dawn and end up staying and playing until dinner.

There is something special about living in a marina community. The "getting to know you" part is very brief. Within minutes of meeting, a dive trip would be arranged, a snorkeling excursion planned, or a party organized aboard each other's boats. And best of all, if we found we didn't get along with our neighbors, we'd just pull up anchor and sail away!

After a year in Mexico, it was finally time to move on. The girls had completed a whole grade of school, I competed in a triathlon, Paul helped build an island, and we forged an unlikely friendship with the cast and crew of *Moonshadow*.

With bows pointing towards Guatemala and a three-week head start, we surely thought we'd seen the last of them.

CHAPTER 17

All in the Same Boat

Rio Dulce River, Guatemala

*"There are good ships and wood ships, ships that sail the sea,
but the best ships are friendships, and may they always be."*

—IRISH PROVERB

Motoring slowly out of the Caribbean and into the mouth of Guatemala's Rio Dulce River, we were greeted by the sounds of cicadas and exotic birds. As towering lush green walls closed in on us, I felt like we had entered another world. A group of shirtless local boys paddling a wooden canoe passed by our hulls with barely a glance. It was as if giant catamarans arriving from Alaska were a common occurrence. Looking around, it didn't seem so to me; there wasn't another boat in sight. I had no idea what to expect of this new foreign land. All I knew was that this huge brown river took us further into the jungle and away from the blue of the open ocean.

We had just left Belize hoping to meet up with more "kid boats". Ambergris Caye was one of our favorite stops, but there were very few kids to celebrate Kelsey's third birthday with. Although our toddler was satisfied with a homemade pinata and a serenade by the famous Eileen Quinn who joined us for cake aboard *Ohana*, the girls missed their friends.

As soon as we were safely anchored near the quirky little town of Livingston just outside the river's entrance, the girls ran around on the trampolines, climbed the forestay, and swung from the fender swing. After burning off some energy, it was time to go ashore and clear in. This entailed getting the girls to put on actual clothes again, tidy up, pack our land bag, lower the dinghy, and pray the engine would start on the first pull.

Roaming the town in search of a building that looked like a government office was something of a treasure hunt. It was difficult to distinguish it from other dilapidated huts, but generally, it was the cleanest and most well-kept on the street. There was always that one local guy who was standing ready to give a tour of "his" town.

"Laundromat, store, garbage." He'd point and kindly grab our smelly trash bags we had been stowing in our forward hatch for weeks. We tipped him generously.

It was customary to clear in 24 hours upon arrival, and all of us had to be present. Kelsey and Madison quickly adapted to this routine, putting on their best dresses and stuffing their backpacks with a toy or book to keep them busy. We all learned to be patient in these countries as government inefficiency seemed to be common everywhere.

Customs and immigration offices were often decorated with flags, a few plastic chairs, and a framed photo on the wall of their current leader. This building ticked all the boxes. While Paul presented passports and arrival documents, I'd sit with the girls and look around for anything to keep them preoccupied for the next hour. They always managed to find something to play with. Kelsey took a spyglass everywhere, and the two of them would examine every nook and cranny of their surroundings like little detectives trying to solve a mystery.

"Do you think we'll see kids here?" Maddi asked as she walked out proudly inspecting the fresh new stamp in her booklet.

"Oh, I'm sure you'll meet lots of new friends here!" I said looking around for anyone shorter than my waist. The girls never minded being just with us, but after long passages they looked forward to sharing stories and playing games again with a new batch of little sailors.

We left Livingston early the following morning to make the 27-mile-long river journey to Mario's Marina at Lake Izabal, a popular stop for cruisers heading to Panama. Our plan was to tour parts of the country for the next week, visiting ruins, temples, markets, and museums.

Paul and I were surprised to see so many sailboats tied along the docks here already. Several cruisers sat in the marina restaurant enjoying the shade of its thatched roof and a long-awaited Wi-Fi. The girls waved at a group of young local boys, some as small as Kelsey, paddling down the river. Families lived along the banks in tiny dwellings haphazardly made from scraps of corrugated metal. Their only means of transport were these carved-out *cayucos,* or skillfully crafted tree trunks.

The laid-back atmosphere had a backpacker's vibe with the promise of hamburgers, local beer, and a strong-enough signal to send overdue emails and blog posts.

As we walked the pier back to *Ohana,* I had Maddi read off the names from the back of boat transoms. Unrecognizable to us, many had hailed from as far as Germany, Australia, and South Africa—most likely making their way around the globe.

Turning the corner, I had to blink a few times to clear my vision. Paul and I looked at each other, eyes wide in disbelief. The familiar labyrinth of gas cans, netting, sarongs, dive gear, and clothing could only mean one boat . . . *Moonshadow!*

"How in the world did they get here before us?" I said out loud, completely shocked. And then we heard it—the chirpy voice that could only be . . .Sheira!

"Oh, my goodness! *Ohana*, my darlings!" She cried running towards us, smiling her twinkly smile. Her leathery, tanned arms made their way around all of us. The rest of her family soon emerged from behind swinging pots and a bunch of bananas hanging from the bimini top. "*Ohana!*" They all shouted, scrambling off their boat to greet us.

Come to find after we left, they simply packed up as well and kept right on going, choosing not to stop in Belize. It was an unexpected reunion, and the girls were thrilled to have the companionship.

For 10 days, our families explored the mighty Rio Dulce River by kayak and horseback riding through dense jungle, greeting villagers and handing out gifts. We toured the Spanish colonial fort, the Castillo di San Felipe de Lara, built in 1644 to stop pirates from entering the lake from the Caribbean. We dove off rocky cliffs, swam under fresh waterfalls, collected tadpoles, and paddled through remote inlets while all four girls sang one Disney song after another.

It was time once again to say goodbye. This happens often in the sailing world—tearful hugs and farewells only to reunite unexpectedly in another port of call. "Hey! Didn't we meet on that beach in Georgetown?" Or "Are you that family from Alaska?"

One thing I loved about traveling together was experiencing the diverse communities and exposing the girls to a wide variety of people. Sailors came from all walks of life—like-minded people in search of adventure, simplicity, and a newfound sense of freedom. Even though our backgrounds, philosophies, dress, and parenting styles were vastly different from those of Moonshadow's, both of our families prioritized one thing… our children.

And that was enough.

CHAPTER 18

Bare Necessities

Lake Atitlan, Guatemala

"Now is no time to think of what you do not have.
Think of what you can do with what there is."

—ERNEST HEMINGWAY

Our driver had a name tag, a van, and a friendly face.

Seems legit, I thought as I hopped in the back with the girls.

No sooner had Paul jumped in the front seat, than the vehicle peeled out from the hotel entrance and onto the main road.

Were we being chased? I wondered, looking at the cloud of dust behind us. Our Guatemalan guide took hairpin corners so fast I thought we would surely career down a cliff. Paul was able to communicate with our guide in Spanish asking him to slow down, *por favor*, several times. He would just smile and proudly continue sharing his favorite sights along the way. We gave up and just held on. For three terrifying hours I clung

SAILING OHANA

to Madison and Kelsey strapped in with the only frayed seatbelt, pulling it across the three of us.

To ease my car sickness, I tried focusing on the giant cross violently swaying from the rearview mirror. That offered little help.

I read the brochure to the girls to help calm my nerves.

"Lake Atitlan is a body of water in a massive volcanic crater in Guatemala's southwestern highlands. With steep verdant hills, it is known for its Mayan villages where vendors sell tradi . . ."

Before I could finish, the van came to a screeching halt.

"*Adios. Gracias!*" Paul said, handing our driver some *quetzales*, coins in the Guatemalan currency. Quickly jumping out, we thanked him and found our way to the boat dock. Our next mode of transport was a wooden launch suitable for about 15 people. What it lacked in comfort, it made up for in speed. *Great, it just keeps getting better,* I thought.

"Look, Mommy, what are those things?" Madison asked, pointing to what looked like tiny dots lined up along the river's edge. As we got closer, I noticed many people working side by side along the shore. Women and children were washing clothes, laying wet garments out to dry on rocks. *What a different world,* I thought. I would never take a laundry room for granted ever again.

The arduous hour-long trip across this massive lake was worth it. The town of Panajachel, or "Pana," was just as described—colorful and bustling, with cobblestone streets lined with food, goods, and artwork handmade by indigenous people of the region. To avoid a meltdown, we made lunch our first stop. The smell of authentic dishes filled the warm air from a restaurant courtyard adorned with trailing bougainvillea. While the kids ordered Chiles Rellenos and Pupusas, I ordered the special of the day, *frijoles negros.*

"You're ordering black beans in Guatemala?" Paul questioned my judgment with a raised eyebrow. Having noticed chickens roaming the

78

entrance, I figured ordering beans would spare an unlucky bird from the chopping block.

After our hearty lunch, Paul paid the check, while I grabbed my heavy salt-encrusted backpack, slinging it over my shoulder.

I've been teased by how much stuff I bring with me everywhere, but when something's needed, I almost always have it. When traveling with small children, I knew to anticipate unforeseen events and pack accordingly. Today was no exception, given we were so far from *Ohana*.

As we made our way to the main street, we blended into a sea of bodies—European tourists, ex-pats, sailors, backpackers, and locals with baskets balanced on their heads swarmed around us. Kelsey found a safe place on Paul's shoulders to get a better view of the action rather than everyone's knees.

I was admiring some colorful wool blankets when suddenly I doubled over with stomach cramps. *Oh, no! The black beans!* I winced in pain.

"Paul, babe." I whispered. "I need to go . . . *now!*"

"What? Where?" He noticed me clutching my sides. "Uh, oh, I knew it!" Putting his arm around me, Paul swiveled around looking for any building that might have a toilet. Still holding Kelsey's little ankles, he pointed to an alley not far from where we were standing.

"Maybe try over there," he said shrugging. An old man sat on a stool; a sleeping dog laid at his feet. *Hmmm, unlikely,* I thought as I weaved through the crowd.

"Stay right here!" I yelled back to my family.

"*¿Donde esta el baño?*" I asked the man with desperate urgency.

Without even looking up, he pointed a gnarled finger down the passageway. There was a large barrel next to him with a tin can on top and a pile of papers next to it.

"*¡Gracias!*" I shouted back, breaking into a sprint. As the brick walls got narrower, I discovered a broken door hanging off its hinges leading to another room with three elevated holes in the floor. *This must be it!* I fumbled around. With seconds to spare, I realized what was missing.

"*Oh, no!*" I said out loud, rummaging through my backpack at my feet. *You've got to be kidding me. How could I not pack toilet paper?* I removed a protein bar, a Band-Aid, insect repellent, a bottle of water, and sunscreen from my bag. Nothing remotely useful. Frantically looking around, I realized what the man outside had on his table—napkins! I quickly put myself back together and shuffled back to him.

"*Cinco quetzales,*" he said, with a gentle smile, surely knowing I'd be back. I gave him a few coins, grabbed a handful, and ran. I got back just in time.

Looking around, I reminded myself to be more careful about what I ate in foreign countries. Most importantly, to never travel without this important necessity.

The concrete room was bare. No mirror. No sink. I felt a rush of gratitude for the people of this country. Their resourcefulness was admirable, as was their kindness and generosity. Seeing how other people lived and adjusted to their circumstances was something we wanted our daughters to appreciate and humbly respect.

On *Ohana*, we washed our clothes in a little plastic tub, hanging them out to dry from the lifelines. We often took rain showers, rationed water, and wasted nothing. Living on a boat was a huge transition for all of us, but we quickly learned to adapt.

We baked our own bread, made toys out of boxes, mixed our own milk and fished for our dinner.

By welcoming a life of simplicity, we had chosen to live more deeply and intentionally, with more breath-taking moments than we could have ever thought possible.

As I walked back out and into the sunshine, I smiled, thanking the kind old man on the stool and gave his dog a pat on the head.

For all I knew, he could have been the richest man in Guatemala.

CHAPTER 19

Pirates of the Caribbean

Cayos Vivorillo, Honduras

"What did the ocean say to the pirate?
Nothing. It just waved."

When I think of pirates, names like Jack Sparrow, Captain Hook, and Black Beard come to mind. The plunderous fictional characters with hooks for hands and wide-brimmed hats are easily identifiable and the only ones I'd like to meet on the high seas.

A new brand of pirate was out there, however . . . definitely few and far between, but still a concern as we made our way through this lonely route off the coast of Honduras.

Before we left Alaska, Paul and I talked about what sort of personal protection to have onboard. It seemed a gun would be the smartest choice, but constantly declaring a weapon and having it held by customs officials sounded like just another hurdle and hassle. We wanted neither.

Whenever we found ourselves anchored alone, my Spidey-sense started tingling. At night as my family slept, I'd lie awake trying to make out any unfamiliar noise. I'd create scenes in my head of what we would do should any unwanted visitor try to get on board. If friendly attempts failed, plan B included flare guns, butane torches, or a fishing gaff. I kept a small can of aerosol hairspray next to my bed . . . just in case. I had to get creative.

After an adventurous week in the Bay Islands, Honduras, we set a course to Panama. To get a fair and safer distance off the coast of Nicaragua, we decided to anchor off in Cayos Vivorillo, a common stop for cruisers making this passage. Located 70 miles offshore, these tiny specks of land are so small they don't even show up on a map of the Caribbean Sea. This knowledge made our position that much more isolating.

Although our days at anchor here were calm and uneventful, I was on edge. It was so remote. My thoughts kept turning to the family that had been murdered on their sailboat in this exact location a few years earlier. The sole caretaker on the island gave me little comfort as he stood in a loincloth staring out at us. We made friends with this nonverbal man who had intentionally positioned himself on this sandbar for a year, living like a castaway. Nevertheless, he kindly offered us coconuts, lobbing off the top with his machete before handing the four of us our refreshments. In turn we gave him some fishing lures.

After two days of snorkeling and building "touch tanks" with the girls in the surrounding coral-laden reef, we pulled anchor and set sail for our next big adventure—the Panama Canal transit. As our island friend stood waving from the shore, my foreboding fear of the unknown returned. Time to sharpen the steak knives.

Sure enough, only eight hours after leaving our secluded anchorage, we spotted them a mile away, motoring north as we were proceeding south. Through the binoculars, the large white trawler was loaded with small fishing canoes and about 40 or more tough-looking men lounging on deck.

The 80-foot steel boat came closer and closer. Paul called over the radio. "Northbound vessel approaching sailing catamaran *Ohana* off your port bow, please respond."

Nothing. Paul began a slow turn to the right to make more distance between us. As he turned, they turned. And then, my stomach turned.

"Take the girls down below and stay with them." he said sternly.

At this point, the men on the approaching boat could see into our cockpit and assess our crew. More reason for a blonde woman and two children to stay out of sight.

After several unsuccessful attempts at making radio contact, my pulse raced with dread. Looking out at nothing but the ocean, I immediately thought of scenes from the movie, *Dead Calm*. Remembering that they used flares to defend themselves, I grabbed the plastic case from under the helm station.

As we turned to make some distance, they intentionally closed in on us. Paul kept an eye on all standing watch from the helm as they came within a boat length of our port hull. My adrenaline surged. I've never been so afraid in my life. As I peered out of the salon window, I saw a mass of weather-beaten dark faces scowling at us as they bore down on our boat.

Paul stood his ground, shoulders back. At that very moment all he could think to do instinctively was . . . wave.

And then the most amazing thing happened. All forty men broke out in the biggest, brightest smiles I had ever seen. Not speaking, they all just stood on deck grinning and waving. Paul returned the greeting enthusiastically. This waving went on for about ten seconds. Without a word exchanged, their transom swiftly slipped to the north, and we continued on our way unscathed. I returned to the cockpit with the girls just in time to see their boat disappear over the horizon.

"Well, that was interesting!" Paul hugged us all tightly. He was shaking. I was almost in tears.

We figured them to be a boat full of curious fishermen miles offshore looking for a little entertainment. They certainly gave us more than that.

I was just happy I didn't have to use up my can of hairspray.

CHAPTER 20

Just Passing Through

Panama Canal, Panama

"When one door closes, another opens."

—ALEXANDER GRAHAM BELL

"Can't go over it, can't go under it, got to go through it!" Our girls would sing as we fendered off our boat in preparation for the transit. We had made it to the Panama Canal—one of the seven wonders of the world and gateway into the unknown Pacific.

Boats from all over the world gather here each spring to begin what would be the greatest adventure for many. What a thrill it was traveling in the well-worn wakes of many famous navigators!

Paul hopped in the dinghy to scope out the anchorage and look for familiar boats—preferably those with kids aboard. He spotted a new, beautiful sloop with two boys running around the deck. This was *La Novia*. Little did we know we'd become lifelong friends.

After checking in, we made arrangements for an agent to assist with all of the paperwork, provide additional fenders and lines as well as assign us our point man—a one-eyed 60-year-old named Dracula. It seemed that everyone in the islands had a clever nickname, and the girls certainly got a kick out of his. Dracula was to be our driver, arrange our crew, find four 100-foot dock lines, and make sure we didn't get into any trouble. I'm not sure we were the ones he had to worry about.

His first piece of advice was, "never ever be alone in Colon without Dracula."

We would soon find out why.

After many documents were processed and a hefty fee paid to get ahead of the other boats, we had him drive us into town to go to the bank as well as the grocery store. We needed a big provision as I was assigned galley slave for the entire transit. It would take more than a few cans of Spam to satisfy our big crew of eight.

As we drove beyond the gates of the Panama Yacht Club, we noticed a bus burning outside, with 55-gallon drums also on fire. Without a word, Dracula kept driving, as if that were a normal everyday thing. He swerved quickly to a stop. "Let's go, family! Stay with Dracula!" He was already forging ahead of us, head swiveling. Moving through town was like walking through the Wild West. Tumbleweeds rolled along the street, mangy dogs limped everywhere; dirt and garbage were piled up along fences. And here we were, strolling into the bank with our two children escorted by this strange man named after a monster with poor vision. *What could possibly go wrong?*

After getting our cash safely stowed in our backpack, we made our way through the crowded street back to Dracula's 1972 Toyota.

"What's up with your tires? They look pretty thin." Paul inspected the completely bald wheels.

"Don't worry man, we'll be just fine," Dracula replied, helping the kids into the backseat before zipping off to the grocery store. Weaving in and out of traffic, we finally came to a stoplight. A guy on the side of the road was throwing garbage out of his car and straight into our open window. Immediately, Dracula got out, stomped over to the vehicle, and had words with the man, who continued to dump his trash on the road. Sweltering in the unairconditioned car, we all sat staring at the two of them arguing.

"Dracula, please don't do anything crazy," Paul said under his breath.

Luckily, our driver returned just as the light turned green. We sped off to the grocery store, Dracula shaking his head angrily as he drove. No sooner had we pulled out onto the road, than we heard a loud *bang!* The front tire had exploded. Stopping to assess the damage, Dracula walked around the car, threw up his hands and yelled, "Hop out family! I'll have someone come pick you up in five minutes!"

Jumping into another car, he was gone before we were able to say, "But wait, I thought you said—"

Here we were, a clean-cut American family clad in polo shirts and khakis with a backpack full of cash, standing on the side of the road in Colon doing the very thing we were told not to do.

True to his word, Dracula sent a friend and in less than 10 minutes, a car pulled over to pick us up. As the dust settled, the driver quickly shuffled us into the backseat and sped off to the market.

We bought what the four of us could carry back to *Ohana* from the store and returned to the Yacht Club safely. After waiting another 20 minutes in the hot sun, we boarded a launch to carry us and our 15 bags of food back to our boat. Needless to say, we were ready to get out on the big blue and away from this crazy city!

Our transit number was finally called a few days later. We woke at 3 a.m. to make our way to the canal lock by 5 a.m. My brother-in-law,

Gary, had flown in from Florida to give us a hand with the lines and experience this once-in-a-lifetime event. He, Paul, Dracula, and two other assigned helpers sat in the cockpit, going over the entire process. My job was to see that the crew was fed and happy. Blurry eyed and undercaffeinated, I made a huge, hearty, bacon, egg, and cheese casserole, poured the coffee, and got the girls ready.

Paul started the engines and pulled anchor. We made our way toward the gigantic lock ahead of us. A huge tanker went first and took up the entire canal. *Ohana* was dwarfed by this massive Panamanian ship blocking out much of our sunlight for several hours. Our catamaran was wedged between towering concrete walls—sea levels rising to dizzying heights. The sudden enclosure from the world felt claustrophobic. The yelling, running, and throwing of heavy lines was chaotic. I moved the girls inside where it was safe and quiet, retrieving the Legos from our little toy compartment. As we built a replica of the canal with the colorful building blocks, I explained to the girls what was happening around us.

"The canal is a waterway 80 kilometers long that connects the Atlantic Ocean with the Pacific Ocean. We are going through the first lock and the gates will close behind us. We'll continue going through two more locks, then the last gate will close and another one will reopen and ta-da! We'll be in the Pacific Ocean!"

My simple explanation seemed to satisfy even our toddler who watched in awe as the massive steel doors closed on the final lock. Together we witnessed the last crack of light disappear behind us. We were on the other side!

That same evening, we passed under the impressive 5,007-foot-long Bridge of the Americas. Our arrival in Balboa was highlighted by a visit to the museum and a celebration dinner out with our crew. Dracula and the entire team of line handlers made the whole event an unforgettable experience.

We walked with Gary as he got a cab back to the airport while the girls rode their Razor scooters along the dock. By midnight, we finally collapsed in our bunks exhausted after a very long, but unforgettable day.

As the last of those heavy gates closed behind us, we looked forward to an uncertain future. We had no idea what lay ahead, how big the ocean was, where we might go, or who we would meet.

But our Panama Canal adventure was proof that together we could get *through* anything.

CHAPTER 21

Sealed with a Kiss

Somewhere on the Pacific Ocean

"It is the size of one's will that determines success."

—UNKNOWN

We were down to four cans of Dinty Moore stew, seven cans of chicken, three cans of corn, and a package of frozen tortillas.

Although these ingredients made a pretty good taco, I was craving anything that didn't require a can opener. Having been stuck in the doldrums longer than anticipated, we were still a few days from making landfall in the Galapagos Islands. This windless area of the Pacific, known as The Intertropical Convergence Zone, can make even the most patient sailor go a little crazy. We made the best use of this time making tie-dye T-shirts, baking pretzels, practicing our talent show skits and I finally read all 1192 pages of *Atlas Shrugged*.

I took the midnight to 4 a.m. watch that night. I couldn't wait to finish the season finale of the series *24* we had brought with us on DVD. The little buzz from the egg timer in the galley told me it was my turn on deck. I pressed the light button on my Ironman watch—11:45 p.m. Half asleep, I slid down from the bunk, tied my hair back, and shuffled up the three steps to the salon. Paul gave me a recap of the evening's activity, our position, and wind direction. I gave him a quick kiss goodnight and checked on the girls as I did before every shift. Tonight, they were cuddled together, having talked earlier of having a "sleepover." I found them intertwined—legs, arms, and stuffed animals everywhere. It always amazed me how our kids could sleep through the loud pounding of waves against the hull as we sliced through the water at 8 knots. Gently pulling their blanket up, I secured the hatch overhead as a little sea spray found its way in.

I curled up in my usual cozy corner of the dinette couch. With as much time as I knew we'd spend around the table, the plush sueded upholstery was a comfortable choice for our bare legs. Before I settled in to spend the next four hours with Keifer Sutherland, I looked in the galley pantry for something to snack on; nothing but canned peaches and a bag of dried lentils.

Oh, well, I'll survive. What would Shackleton do?

Whenever we were stuck in a less-than-desirable situation, this was my go-to phrase and reminder for me to toughen up. Ernest Shackleton was best known for his Antarctic expedition where he, his men and ship, *The Endurance,* got stranded in the ice during a discovery mission. For two years they fended off disease and escaped predators while Shackleton ensured the safety of the entire crew. He eventually ate his dogs. I would survive without a cookie.

Every 10 minutes, I'd peek outside and see that all was well. No lights, no odd sounds. Good sign.

An hour into my watch, my stomach rumbled louder than the engines. I paused the show, sat up, and looked around the boat. *There's got to be something yummy around here!*

I thought about all the nooks and crannies where I hid things for special occasions, holidays, and birthdays.

I crept down to the workroom where tools, schoolbooks and crafts were stored. I saw that the girls had gotten into the red and pink construction paper. They had cut out about 50 hearts and were stringing them together. Then I remembered—the Hershey's Kisses!

I had purchased the chocolates back in Panama City to celebrate Valentine's Day. I had asked Paul to put them someplace cool so they wouldn't melt and to hide them from the girls.

Stumbling in the dark, I opened every drawer and compartment and even our ditch kit. I peered under bunks and behind our small bookshelf. I searched in between towels, and under the crew bunk mattress. I passed the electrical panel, making sure the running lights were on so other boats could see us. All good. I had all but given up before I did a double take, looking back at the switchboard again. Four screws held the metal frame in place. Something about it made me think of a safe. *A safe holds valuable things*, I thought. I ran back to the tool drawer and got out a screwdriver. I couldn't contain my excitement as I carefully turned the tiny screws.

Tucking them in my shorts pocket, I unlatched the door and after some gentle jiggling, it gave way. I stared at the labels on each that were glued to the backing to identify each switch. *This is dumb. Why would Paul hide candy in the electrical pan . . .?*

Then I saw it.

A hollow space revealed the corner of a package. I reached my hand inside, carefully pinching the plastic between my fingers. Lo and behold, there it was! The family-size bag of Hershey's Kisses! Wrapped in shiny silver, their little tags gave me a congratulatory wave. I could not believe it! My persistence paid off—I had solved the chocolate kiss mystery!

A trail of tiny wadded-up foil balls exposed my little caper the next morning. Paul was equally shocked and impressed by my determination.

Shackleton would have been proud!

CHAPTER 22

Wild Kingdom

Santa Cruz Island, Galapagos

"It is not the strongest of the species that survive,
nor the most intelligent, but the one most responsive to change."

—CHARLES DARWIN

As a child growing up in the '70s, Sundays meant pancake breakfasts, getting dressed up for church, and The Wonderful World of Disney. After a full day of playing, my brother, sisters, and I would sprawl out on the carpet in front of our old TV console with popcorn and pillows, ready for that magical castle to appear on the screen. But first, we had to wait for my dad's nature show to end—*Mutual of Omaha's Wild Kingdom*. I remember watching an episode with him once featuring the Galapagos Islands. Fascinated by the incredible wildlife—giant tortoises, penguins, and iguanas—I was intrigued by the marine sanctuary's remoteness, only visited by famous explorers like Jacques Cousteau.

Someday I will see the Galapagos, I promised myself.

And there I was, 25 years later, standing on a grassy cliff overlooking Santa Cruz Bay, my family by my side. Smiling, I couldn't help but think back to that moment.

I took Kelsey's little hand, who had wandered too close to the edge. She was trying to get a look at some nesting birds making tiny homes in the rock face.

Upon entering the anchorage in Puerto Ayora, we were greeted by the welcoming barks of sea lions. They were everywhere—in the water, lazing around on boats, and even guarding the door of the local bank.

We received a cruising permit, or *autografo,* prior to arriving. Once cleared in, we were excited to meet up with our friends from *La Novia* for some island adventures.

Much to our surprise, there was a pizza restaurant and ice cream shop in town, so of course, we made that our first stop. With vanilla and chocolate running down their arms, the kids ran around the waterfront playground, burning off a week of cooped-up energy. After a short walk to the visitors' center, we booked a tour of Isabela Island for the following day to snorkel and sightsee. Meanwhile, a local boy offered to take us on an informal tour which really meant, "hop in the back of my pickup. For 50 dollars I'll take you to see the giant tortoises."

As all eight of us bounced through potholes along a narrow dirt road, we passed flocks of pink flamingos, red prehistoric-looking land iguanas, giant cacti, and sleepy Galapagos tortoises dozing in the sun. Madison, Kelsey, Thomas, and George sang songs as they did on every land excursion, drowning out the noise of the vehicle's rumbling engine.

After a week of hiking, swimming, and exploring this enchanting nature preserve, Paul was antsy to get moving. The big blue was out there waiting.

Our ocean passage lay just beyond the breakwater. My anxiety for the long crossing crept back in. I struggled to shake the dreaded feeling of being at sea for three weeks. To clear my head, Catherine and I took our kids to play on the black volcanic rocks. As we watched them chase the red crabs around, we shared our apprehension for the journey ahead of us.

"At least you don't have these two!" she laughed as we watched her boys wrestle in the tide pools. "Maybe I should just tether them to the cockpit table!" she said jokingly pulling Thomas' board shorts back up. Catherine and I wouldn't see each other until we met again in the Marquesas Islands. I would miss the companionship of other women for a while, but I was ready to move on as well.

After we stocked up at the local grocery store, *Ohana* was ready with fresh food, water, and fuel. At least our boat was prepared for this big adventure.

I glanced around the harbor while bringing in the anchor. As the chain tucked itself neatly in the locker, I gazed beyond at the sunbathing sea lions and pelicans standing guard at the channel entrance. I reminded myself about the many people who came before us, crossing oceans often with nothing but a sextant. We could do this.

Securing the anchor, I made a circular motion with my finger, signaling to Paul that we were clear to move. He motored out slower than usual as the girls were jumping on the trampolines waving goodbye to the wildlife.

"Bye, crabs! Bye, turtles! Bye-bye, blue-footed boobies!" they giggled.

As soon as we were out of the channel, the choppy seas returned along with the knot in my stomach. We all met back in the cockpit. Paul gave me a big reassuring hug before taking the girls inside to safely play. He liked to navigate from his comfortable leather chair. I remained outside at the helm station watching the last speck of land disappear behind us. *Here we go.*

3,000 nautical miles of open ocean lie ahead.

It was the most humbling moment of my entire life.

CHAPTER 23

Weather or Not

Pacific Ocean

"Life isn't about waiting for the storm to pass.
It's about learning how to dance in the rain."

—VIVIAN GREENE

B lackness all around me.

It engulfed our boat quickly. This nightly show never got old. The sky traded its daylight for a spectacular orange, purple, and pink grand finale. Fumbling for the round knob on the side of my headlamp, I turned it on, the little bulb casting a surprisingly bright beam ahead of me.

I stumbled over Kelsey's tiny rubber Crocs as I made my way inside. Picking them up, I stored them neatly in the shoe bin under the step.

"Beep, beep, beep." The radar alarm had gone off from the nav station inside. Paul had set the guard zone wider than usual for my night watch. He knew I liked plenty of warning in the unlikely event that we would meet up with another vessel. A tiny dot appeared on the screen. I made note of its location.

Guiding my fingers along the settee in the dark, I was tempted to crawl into the corner and bury my head in the pillows where it was quiet and warm. However, being outside in the cockpit kept me in touch with our surroundings, shifts in weather, and anything out of the ordinary. I never wanted to miss a thing.

It was day 12—a week out from our arrival into Hiva Oa in the Marquesas. But we weren't counting; in fact, we wanted to slow it down. For us, sailing didn't mean racing; it was simply an adventurous way of getting from one place to the other, enjoying the easy pace of life on the ocean while experiencing each day as it unfolded. Being surrounded by water on all sides forced us to notice anything and everything—changes in wind patterns, a new cloud, its shape, whether it would bring rain. Surprise visits from dolphins, whales, or flying fish broke up our otherwise consistent daily routines.

It was amazing what could be accomplished in a 24-hour day with no phones or electronics to distract us from fully living in our environment. Cooking, playing games, instruments, reading, building, writing, fixing, creating, cleaning, dancing, baking, or simply watching the waves were some of the many things we'd do to pass the time. Aside from book-keeping and correspondence with managers, we were free to do whatever we wanted.

With nothing but ocean in every direction, I often felt like we were the only ones on the planet. It was incredibly peaceful and a little unnerving as well.

Being on watch while my family slept was a huge responsibility I took very seriously. If I did sleep at all, I dozed for a few minutes a time, worried that we'd drift off course or worse yet, hit something.

I reset the radar alarm and checked our surroundings. No lights, nothing around for miles. Peeking my head into our cabin, I crept down the few teak steps to see if Paul was sleeping. I didn't dare wake him; he needed solid rest for his 4 to 8 a.m. watch. *I can handle this*, I thought grabbing a hoodie and a handful of saltines. Turning off my headlamp, I scanned both port and starboard and then on tiptoe looking over the canvas bimini top as I did every 20 minutes of my four-hour watch. The dark sky merging with ink-black water made me feel as though we were sailing into a void. Except for the faint glow of the galaxy above, we were moving along in a liquid abyss. Nothing, not a soul for hundreds of miles, day in and day out.

I settled myself back into the corner of the cockpit, propping up the pillow I had grabbed from our bunk. We were motor sailing along at a steady seven knots, our autohelm humming away. A cool breeze brushed past my face; I enjoyed its company as if it were a visitor passing through. I'd meditate on each passing wave, reflecting on life and how blessed we were to experience this.

Before we started our journey, I would gaze out from the safety of the shore watching the tide roll in and out, wondering what lay beyond. I'd see a ship on the horizon and think, *what a slow way to get anywhere.* From an airplane, our boat was just a tiny speck to the naked eye. In six hours, those passengers would be in Bora Bora, sipping pina coladas. *Soon that will be us,* I thought. Just another thousand miles.

The little egg timer next to my head startled me. The ring was loud enough to alert me, but quiet enough that it didn't wake the girls.

I sat up, groggy, my environment unchanged except for a slight shift in the wind. The telltales were crossing over each other. I eased off the jib sheet until they flew straight again. Settling back against the cushion, I looked up, noticing the milky way in all its grandeur, a magic show just for me. I contemplated so much during these watches—where would we call home again? What did our future have in store for us? Like the ocean, there are simply some things I couldn't control . . . our future was one of them. I decided to lay back and enjoy this perfect moment . . . on autopilot.

Nibbling on my crackers, I pulled the hood over my head, tying the ends tight around my chin. The breeze was back and filled the sails.

The waves glided smoothly along our hulls, familiar and comforting like a lullaby. I drifted off again.

"Beep, beep, beep!" There it was again. I checked the radar, the black dot less than a mile or so from our boat.

I strained to see a masthead or red and green running lights from the front hatch, anything that resembled another vessel out here. Nothing but blackness. *Hmm, strange.* Returning to the cockpit, that's when I smelled it. The heavy, earthy scent followed by a chill could only mean one thing . . . rain! Without warning, it came down like a waterfall. *"Squall!"* I hollered down to Paul, who appeared on deck so fast it was like seeing a ghost.

He moved quickly, idling down the engines, bringing the sails in while I secured all the hatches inside. It was an unspoken dance we had done many times before. The black dot had been an isolated thundershower so dense it could be picked up on the radar. I checked on our girls, making sure they were warm and dry. Surprisingly, they kept right on sleeping.

After the storm cell passed, Paul reset the guard zone, checked our surroundings, and made his way down below. "You all right out here, hon?"

"Yep, all good," I replied, drying off with a beach towel. I was anxious to get back to my quiet time.

Turning off my headlamp, I found a dry spot under the bimini top, sinking low in the pillow for the duration of my shift. The parting clouds revealed a clear black sky. The air smelled fresh and alive. I felt that way too. I focused my eyes on a single bright star.

It acknowledged me with a twinkle.

CHAPTER 24

The Soccer Ball

Fatu Hiva, French Polynesia

"What divides us pales in comparison to what unites us."

—TED KENNEDY

We were off by an hour.

Calculating wind speed, knots of current and sea conditions were all factors when leaving one place for the other. Oftentimes our days would start at 5 a.m. to cover as much ground as possible to arrive before nightfall, which is always preferable.

Motoring into the Hana Vave Bay after dark was like threading a needle with your eyes closed. Without any moon or light on shore to guide us, we carefully idled back on the throttle, straining to hear the pounding surf against the nearby towering cliff faces.

Fatu Hiva is the southernmost isolated island of the Marquesas in French Polynesia. While most of our cruising company sailed on to the Tuamotus, Paul and I wanted to venture off and visit this gem once explored by Thor Heyerdahl. The Norwegian scientist was notable for his Kon-Tiki expedition in 1947, in which he sailed 8,000 km across the Pacific Ocean in a hand-built raft from South America to the Tuamotu islands. His best-selling book, *Kon-Tiki,* still rests on our bookshelf, worn and read many times over. To make a stop here was a once-in-a-lifetime experience.

With nothing but sound to guide us, we dropped our hook in the middle of the anchorage based on the volume and tone of the waves. As Paul set the anchor alarm, I sat in the cockpit adjusting my eyes to the darkness. Looming shapes around our boat were the sides of craggy mountains, way too close for comfort.

Maddi and Kelsey, having been tucked in earlier, remained fast asleep as always. Paul and I slept restlessly, waking to check our position every hour. There wasn't a lot of wiggle room for error.

By the next morning, we woke to what looked like a scene from *Jurassic Park*. Ragged green spires soared high above the tiny anchorage. Impressed with our blind anchoring skills, Paul still wanted to move *Ohana* more in the center of the bay. We assumed there would be others arriving and wanted a wide berth away from the rocks as well. Kelsey, almost always the first one up, made her way to the bow to see where in the world she was. Hoisting her onto my hip, we stood awestruck, taking it all in.

A wonderful classic by Herman Melville, *Typee,* describes the wild and remote South Pacific islands and remains one of our favorite books. Nothing, however, could prepare me for this level of beauty. To be anchored there, standing on the deck of our boat like one of the great navigators was surreal. I can see why Heyerdahl made this his island home for so many years. For anyone wanting to get out of civilization, this would be the place.

"I wanna do it, Daddy!" Kelsey shouted, wriggling out of my arms, and running to the foredeck. Paul wanted to reposition *Ohana* before we headed to shore. Hanging on to her daddy's leg, she stepped on the anchor windlass button once he gave her the go-ahead.

Picking up the binoculars, I panned the shore making out a dirt road and a few structures. A small white church with a tall steeple marked the center of the village, a welcoming sight.

Once we felt secure, we dinghied to the gray, pebbly beach. Without a single soul to greet us, it was as if we really had this island to ourselves.

We found the road that took us around the town. The girls had brought their soccer ball, kicking it down the path as we strolled along. We passed a tiny post office, what looked like a school, and a few modest dwellings. I was surprised to see a woman, the first sign of life, hanging wash out to dry. *"Bonjour!"* We greeted her warmly, offering small gifts I had put in my backpack. She was overjoyed with simple hair accessories and a new lipstick.

In exchange, she gave us a handful of oranges and breadfruit. She didn't speak a word, but smiled and waved goodbye as though we were old friends. As we carried on, we noticed every tree along the way bore some sort of fruit: limes, coconuts, and mangos. Fragrant jasmine flowers and yellow hibiscus brightened this otherwise verdant island.

A very large, dark-skinned man in nothing but board shorts sat outside in front of his hut. He looked like a statue staring forward until he swatted a fly. As we walked along the lane, he didn't move except to give us a slow nod of acknowledgment.

"Hello mate!" Paul greeted him, raising his hand. My husband used the universal word "mate" to make fast friends anywhere we went. It usually worked unless that person was a giant Polynesian minding his own business. He didn't budge nor did he smile back. I noticed the thatched-roof hut was missing a door. Aside from a straw mat, there wasn't really anything I could see that resembled furnishings inside.

He grunted something in French and pointed to the ball Kelsey clutched tightly in her arms.

"Soccer ball, yes!" Paul replied. The man pointed again aggressively. "Oh! You want it?" Paul said chuckling. *Oh, no, not our soccer ball!* We had dragged this thing all the way from Fort Lauderdale. Kelsey pulled the ball into her chest, not wanting to give it up. I smiled at her nodding. *It's the right thing to do.*

The man stood up and retreated into his dark cave without a word. A minute later, this stoic oversized islander emerged ducking his head under the doorway clearly made for a smaller human. Over his shoulder, he carried a stalk—more like a tree of bananas. He walked over to us and thrust them out for Paul to take. Kelsey, no taller than his shin, reached up and reluctantly handed him the ball.

He turned on his dirty bare heel, tossed the ball into the hut, and plopped himself down on his front step. Without speaking a word, he took a swig from his bottle of Hinano. We continued on our way.

Where we came from, our family had access to a thousand soccer balls. For this man, it may have been his first and only one.

Back onboard, we hung our bananas from a carabiner outside. Kelsey soon forgot about her ball and gained a valuable lesson. Our trades across the Pacific represented friendship—an unspoken thank you for their warm hospitality and generosity.

And for all we knew, we could have given Fatu Hiva their first-ever soccer team.

CHAPTER 25

The Table

*"A single conversation across the table with a wise man
is better than ten years mere study of books."*

—HENRY WADSWORTH LONGFELLOW

Our modest chipped cockpit table, always in need of another sanding and coat of varnish, wasn't megayacht worthy, but for us, it may as well have been.

We have met a wide variety of characters, many still lifelong friends, who have shared their amazing stories, talents, philosophies, and wisdom with us. Who would have thought a girl and boy from humble beginnings would sit with corporate giants, celebrities, pastors, hippies, artists, musicians, high-tech moguls, eccentrics, escapists . . . the list goes on.

During the daytime, *Ohana's* table served as a homeschool desk, an ideal place for a chess game, a craft, or curling up to watch the world go by.

Evenings at sundown, the table would take on an entirely new life. Happy hour with charcuterie boards and rum punches would be enjoyed by those we had just met and invited over, as well as our best passage-making friends from all over the world. Tying their dinghies to the transom, parents and their kids of all ages would step up into the cockpit, offering a unique dish created earlier in their tiny galleys. Freshly caught fish or conch fritters, a secret casserole, or a bottle they'd been saving just for the occasion. With curious heads swiveling, the familiar conversations would begin.

"Wow, is this custom-built? I've never seen a cat this wide," Or "How does she do in heavy weather?" "How much anchor chain do you put out?"

The kids would scatter to the foredeck or down below, excited to see how other little people lived on a boat, bringing a book, a favorite game, or DVD to swap.

Once our guests were given a tour and all settled around the cockpit table, the evenings were often accompanied by an impromptu show. Madison, always the master of ceremonies, would open with "The Star-Spangled Banner," followed by Kelsey's flute solo, a kazoo, or maybe just coconuts clapped together. Visiting boat kids would offer a song, a poem, or a skit that they had just rehearsed down below decked out in random finery they had found to dress up in. The adults would jump in with a talent of their own. And, boy, were there many!

More than a wood centerpiece, our table was a gathering place where one could sit with a stranger one minute and be laughing like old friends the next. It made the perfect kid fort when draped with wet sheets drying in the sun. It was a place to put up your feet while stargazing during long night watches.

How many sunsets would our family experience together at anchor listening to Van Morrison, Norah Jones, or the dreamy crooning of Sarah Dashew? Too many to count.

Charts laid out, adventures planned, dreams made, and stories shared.

It's all about the table.

CHAPTER 26

A Reel Treat

Suwarrow, Cook Islands, South Pacific

"Luck affects everything. Let your hook always be cast;
in the stream where you least expect it there will be a fish."

—OVID

Nothing enhances boat life better than sounds—the bubbling of coffee grounds in the stovetop percolator, the gentle pitter-patter of rain washing the deck clean, an offshore breeze whistling through the rigging or the screaming sound of line peeling off a reel when a fish has taken the bait.

On most long passages, Paul would set up two fishing rods on either side of the cockpit. When the boat was under sail, we employed our trolling technique—dragging two lures through the water in hopes we'd trick a fish to think it was another moving fish. Sometimes we'd bring up piles of seaweed, creatively tangled around the three-pronged hook, other times a little tunny too small to keep. That day was no different . . . or so we thought.

We had just spent two blissful weeks in Tahiti, Moorea, and Bora Bora with Paul's parents, who desperately needed to see their grandchildren – even if it meant crossing the ocean. After swimming with stingrays, beachcombing and playing with the girls, they flew back to Florida content that we were all doing just fine on our seafaring adventures.

Paul and I set a course for Suwarrow, a tiny coral atoll in the Cook Islands, where New Zealander Tom Neale, the famous author of *An Island to Oneself,* lived alone for 16 years. While most cruisers sailed on to Rarotonga, we took the opportunity to experience what life was like on this remote 3-square-mile island before our passage to American Samoa. There were no facilities on this isolated ring-shaped reef, aside from a small, thatched caretaker's hut. The sublime beauty of the untouched coral-laced lagoon merging with blue sky and tropical palms draping over white sand overloaded my senses. Surprisingly, we weren't the only ones who wanted the Robinson Crusoe experience. We met up with several new and old friends and after a week of snorkeling, beach bonfires and fascinating stories shared by our hosts over giant roast crab, it was time to pull anchor. Summer in the Southern Hemisphere was fast approaching, and we were all looking forward to Christmas in New Zealand.

Once we were away, Paul pulled out a colorful plastic wiggly thing from the fish locker just under the helm station. The lure, with its rubbery tentacles and wide eyes, was made to look like a squid, although I've never seen one quite that pink or as terrified.

He secured it to the 800 yards of 90-pound Spectra woven line returning the rod to its holder. After organizing a project for the girls involving wine corks and hot glue, I stepped into the cockpit for some fresh air. I noticed the pole's tip bouncing and bobbing as the bright skirted bait danced through *Ohana*'s wake.

"Do you really think we want to catch something way out here?" I joined him at the helm. I loved fishing, but I knew that anything above

50 pounds may require a babysitter and a lot of fridge space, neither of which we had.

"If anything's gonna happen, Kitty, it's gonna happen out there!" He pointed with a grin, quoting Kurt Russell from the movie *Captain Ron*.

The one thing I loved about Paul was that he was always willing to give something a try.

"Let's see what happens. We'll figure it out," he'd say. "Ready, fire, aim!"

Just two hours into the 500-mile passage to Samoa, we hear the high-pitched scream of fishing line quickly being stripped from our reel.

"*Fish on!*" I yelled. Paul dropped his sandwich mid-bite and sprang into action. He headed the boat up quick to slow us down and fired up the engines. Moving like the Flash, he furled the jib and sheeted the main tight. I jumped to the transom, working the drag as we had rehearsed many times.

Besides Converse high tops, hip waders were my go-to footwear growing up. I knew how to fish. As a child I landed Alaskan king salmon two times my weight and would wake at the crack of dawn to go fly fishing with my dad. But the sound coming from our heavily strained pole was something I had never heard before. This was clearly no salmon.

The girls were taught never to go beyond the cockpit door in certain situations. Most often it was when Paul and I needed to take sails down in heavy weather. In this case, it was to bring in a very large fish. They stayed put and watched the show from the entryway cheering us on.

With *Ohana* slowed to almost a stop, Paul was able to reel in and give the fish a break. I was thankful we added the extra line we needed for just this reason. Paul took over the controls, maneuvering in reverse and forward while I played it for a while. We had no idea how to land something of this size. I watched a fishing show once on the Discovery Channel, but all I remember were a lot of suntanned guys in Pelagic gear and mirrored sunglasses using very high-tech equipment. I think Paul got that old pole from his brother-in-law's shed. I can't be certain, but it didn't give me a whole lot of confidence.

Straddling the side of the cockpit, I sat firmly gripping the fishing rod with my gloved hands. My muscles strained as I brought the monster toward the boat. *Lower the tip, reel like a son of a gun, pull the tip back up, hold, lower the tip, reel like a son of a gun.* My dad's instructions repeated in my head as I continued the fight. Paul tossed me a fishing belt to support the rod more comfortably. Before I wondered where and why we bought such a thing, I happily buckled it around me and went back to my wrestling match.

As I reeled in, Paul slowly reversed. I caught a moment of respite and glanced at our surroundings . . . not a soul anywhere, not a speck of land. For a second, I panicked. The girls! I spun around only to see Maddi and Kelsey giggling in the doorway, taking pictures with our tiny digital camera.

With our biceps burning and sore, we played the beast for 30 minutes before it finally surfaced and began thrashing about. Shark? Swordfish? Marlin? Whatever it was, I wasn't certain we had the proper tools to haul it on deck. Finally, a violent splash and something glistening blue leaped from the water. I gasped. The huge yellowfin tuna flicked its tail, revealing its size. It was a stunning sight, the biggest fish I'd ever seen in my life! *What have we gotten ourselves into*? I thought, wondering if we should cut the line. The tuna disappeared under the boat to take a little rest . . . and so did we.

Quickly doing the calculations, it would take us roughly three full days to get to Pago Pago Harbor. Where would we keep it all? The filets would have to share space with the lettuce, cheese, and remaining apple in our cool box. *Make a salad, store the fish!*

I pulled out the gaff from the fish locker. Switching positions, Paul carefully balanced on the back of the transom ladder, club in one hand, hook in the other ready to strike. If there were ever a time we could lose our captain, this was it!

With the boat's engines in neutral, the glistening creature finally surfaced, tired, and defeated. I reeled in the last bit of slack. As Paul reluctantly, but forcibly knocked the fish over the head, he plunged the gaff into its glistening side. Using every bit of strength, we pulled the beautiful 160-pound yellowfin tuna up onto the deck. Our eyes were as wide as that lucky pink lure.

For a moment, I felt a little remorseful. Such an incredible creature swimming along minding its own business and the next fighting for its life. We all said a little prayer of gratitude over the fish, thanking God for the feast we were about to eat and soon enjoy with others.

Paul, dripping with sweat, managed to drag it into the cockpit. The girls cautiously stepped out to get a closer look. Kelsey held up her plastic tropical fish chart for identification, while Maddi retrieved the offshore fishing manual from our bookshelf.

It was a quick study. I held the page open while Paul read how best to filet our trophy. His eyes went from book to blade to fish and back again. He came from a family who golfs. This was not in his wheelhouse. Like a scene from *Edward Scissorhands,* he managed to cut, slice, and store the raw pink meat into dozens of quart-size baggies. The butchering went on for hours. Madison recreated the event with a song while Kelsey swished about in her purple tutu.

I returned *Ohana* back on course while Paul packed the cool box to the very top. For the duration of the passage, we feasted on fresh sashimi, grilled tuna steaks, tuna casserole, and tuna sandwiches all the way to American Samoa.

Our friends were in for a "reel" treat and the best fish story this side of the equator!

CHAPTER 27

Anchor's Away!

Pago Pago, American Samoa

"Be brave. Take risks. Nothing can substitute experience."

–PAULO COELHO

We had been anchored in Pago Pago, American Samoa, for a week, sharing the rest of our catch with other neighboring boats.

It was time to set a course for Tonga, the last leg of our journey before the hop across the ditch. I wasn't disappointed leaving behind the StarKist tuna processing plant that added to the smell of dumped garbage. I'm not sure if our anchor was held by sand or an old refrigerator door, but whatever it was secured us to the bottom.

A storm was approaching this U.S. territory and we had just finished our final provisioning at the nearby supermarket.

"Well, guess it's time for us to head out!" Paul jotted down the weather updates as they came through over the VHF.

"What? Wouldn't this be the worst time?" I was confused. I was drawing with Kelsey at the table, since it was all we could do to remain upright. Our normally steady catamaran was rocking from the waves already, and we hadn't even left the harbor.

"Oh, but this is the best time!" he replied assuredly. "The winds will also be in our favor heading South to Tonga. We just need to get out of this anchorage by morning. Once we change course it will be a lot calmer."

I looked out the front hatches. White caps were already forming right here inside the anchorage. I could only imagine what conditions would be like beyond the channel!

Earlier, a small group of us had driven our dinghies ashore for a celebratory send-off and to discuss the best time to head out—before or after the storm passed. As the winds kicked up, we knew it was time to get back to our boats and secure our anchors. The kids put out the little bonfire they had made on the concrete wharf. Much to our amazement, they had gathered little sticks, lit a match, and organized a pint-sized party of their own.

"You're crazy to leave in these conditions!" our friend said as he passed our painter line to us and waved goodbye.

"We'll be fine!" Paul replied, "it's just a little sporty!"

Undeterred by the howling winds, he woke me at 6 a.m. to help haul the anchor. I sleepily put on a sweatshirt and baseball cap and shuffled out to the cockpit, where I found him wrestling with something over the bow. I could only see his feet as he leaned over the bridle. The anchor rode had gotten wrapped around a pile of metal, and it took many maneuvers to free us from all the debris. Once away, we dodged the hundreds of plastic bottles that had been blown into the bay. It made me angry seeing such a beautiful place trashed with so much garbage. As lovely as the people on this island were, their waste management was something to be questioned.

Motoring out, the entrance was just what we expected. Roughly 10-foot seas—right on the nose! All the banging woke the kids as they crawled on all fours up the steps to the settee. With each falling wave they'd stand on the cushions, pretending they were surfing.

"Whooooaaaa! Wahoooo!" they yelled lifting their arms over their head like they were on a roller coaster ride.

"Fun, right?" I said sarcastically, grabbing Kelsey, who lost her balance landing on top of her sister. Watching them laughing together, I was grateful for their obliviousness to the rough conditions. Nothing they hadn't been through before. *What I would give for a cup of coffee.* I thought, steadying myself against the table. Once we found calmer seas, I could finally put the kettle on. For now, I'd go without caffeine and ride this out safely.

"Be patient, girls!" Paul shouted. "We'll be out of this in no time!"

After two hours slamming into the gigantic swells, we changed course. The incessant banging instantly stopped. Although the waves remained as tall as skyscrapers, they pushed us forward and we surfed downwind on to our next destination—Nuku'alofa, Tonga—350 nautical miles away.

After about 5 miles in, we shared the news over the VHF with our friends back in the harbor that we had cleared out and were safely on our way.

Paul's friend, Vito, transmitted over the radio. "You were smart to leave when you did, *Ohana!*" He was still moored, assessing the damage in Pago Pago.

Boats that remained in the harbor did not fare well. Several were dragged into other boats, while anchors remained stuck in the tangled mass of garbage. Sailboats that had been tied alongside the dock were pushed together and damaged. From what we heard, it was an unfortunate disaster for many.

Although this experience was a little scary, I was grateful to Paul for understanding the weather, trusting his instincts, and departing when we did.

Since leaving the safety of our land home, we were out of our comfort zone every day, forced to make decisions without overriding the other. Good communication and flexibility were essential but given our stubbornness this was probably our biggest challenge.

We learned a tremendous amount while sailing *Scarlett* together for years before our children were born. If we hadn't done that, I do not believe I would have understood the harsher realities of boat life. Nor would I have been nearly as prepared to include our daughters had I not experienced the level of discomfort that naturally comes with living on the water—the intense togetherness day in and day out, patience for practically everything, the monotony of passage making, marine toilets exploding, the endless slog in search of food, navigating through precarious coral reefs, exhaustion, inconveniences, isolation, the list goes on.

"If it were easy everyone would be doing it," Paul would often say.

"It's the hard that makes it all worthwhile."

CHAPTER 28

The Dress

Ha'apai, Tongatapu, Tonga

*"Enjoy the little things, for one day you may look back
and realize they were the big things."*

—ROBERT BRAULT

From the black shores of Atuona in the Marquesas Islands to the pristine white shores of the Tuamotus, our family was treated to a picture-perfect anchorage every day. After awhile, even the most idyllic stretch of sand could lose its appeal. "Girls, do you want to go explore?" I would ask. "No thanks, we're busy Mama," they'd reply, not even looking up. If a trip to land interfered with their crafts or games, Madison and Kelsey were content to stay on the boat with Dad.

Taking the rare opportunity, I would grab my waist belt and head for the beach to enjoy time by myself. Sometimes I took the kayak or paddleboard, but our dinghy offered me the freedom to explore farther and faster.

Starting the engine after a few pulls, I maneuvered my way around the bay in search of a place to tie up. Discovering an old wooden dock on shore, I quickly tilted the motor to avoid hitting the sand with the propeller and secured a bowline around one of the boards.

Jumping off the inflatable, I took in my surroundings. Not a sound, except for the trill of terns and the gentle rippling of waves against the shore. No matter how many beaches I have been to, I still find myself completely enchanted by each one—my happy place. Shielding my eyes from the sun, I looked out at *Ohana* and smiled.

My whole world was on that boat.

As I walked barefoot along the warm sand, I picked up a few spotted cowrie shells, knowing the girls would make use of them. I had added jewelry pliers and a container of natural hemp twine to our craft bin, and they sure came in handy. The girls had quickly learned how to make creative macrame bracelets and anklets to give as gifts to all their new friends.

Finally looking up, I noticed a barricade blocking me from going further. NO ONE PAST THIS POINT – MEMBERS ONLY, the sign read. *Rats!* I thought, looking at my side littered with debris and over the fence at theirs. Cabanas peppered the perfectly raked grounds, drinks decorated with fruit speared with tiny plastic swords were being carried out to guests basking in swimwear clearly not made for saltwater. Glancing down at my faded string bikini top and macaroni noodle necklace, I knew I didn't stand a chance of getting past this point. For a moment I felt a little like a hobo, an outsider on the opposite side of the fence. I caught the eye of a sunbather who simply ignored me and went back to her novel. *I'd rather be on this side anyway,* I thought as I plucked a rare cone shell from a pile of dried seaweed. I wouldn't have said no to one of those daiquiris though!

After a couple of hours snorkeling and diving, I had a bag full of shells and blue, worn pieces of china tumbled and smoothed by the water and sand. The girls loved this rare "sea pottery" and I couldn't wait to show them my collection.

From the islands of the Bahamas, Caribbean, Central America, and South Pacific on down to New Zealand, the objects found on remote beaches were what really made these places special—the treasures that lie waiting amongst the grains for someone to notice and give purpose to.

One such day was on a beach in the Ha'apai islands in Tongatapu, Tonga. Once Paul tied up the dinghy, we would all disperse. Madison would run off into the brush in search of palm fronds to weave into baskets. Kelsey was our bottle collector—glass, plastic—you name it, she found it, filled it, and repurposed it. As for Paul, he just happily stood on the beach, making sure *Ohana* wasn't dragging. "Hold this, Daddy. Hold this!" The girls would shout, filling the pockets of his cargo shorts.

How life had changed for us since leaving our land home. Our to-do lists now included collecting sticks to support our daughter's make-believe salon on the beach, geocaching for hours in search of hidden objects, or our favorite—collecting trash. Our boat became a floating art gallery. Old toothbrushes and a single flipflop would make the perfect sculpture when held together with Styrofoam and hot glue. Driftwood signs were colorfully painted and put around our boat for welcoming décor. Shell mobiles clinked together in the breeze from the bimini top. Large brown seed pods that dropped from the trees were decorated with beads and feathers making unique musical instruments when shaken. Anything the girls could get their hands on, they would make into something useful and beautiful.

Little Kelsey had the advantage of being low to the ground and spotted it first - a tiny bit of blue and yellow. I noticed from down the beach her tugging on something deeply buried in the packed brown sand.

"What'd you find, babe?" I slowly jogged up to her.

"I dunno! I'm trying to pull it out!" she said with her knees bent in a determined stance. Kelsey barely said a word her first two years, and now at age three, she had the vocabulary of a ten-year-old. Her hair, bleached white from endless days in the sun, was plastered to her sunscreen-covered face. Her tiny arms pulled at something that looked like colorful cloth.

"It looks like a shirt or something!" she squealed, proud of her discovery.

"I think it's a dress! Mommy, it's a dress!"

"It sure is, honey. I wonder where it came from?" I glanced around looking for any sign of life.

"I dunno, maybe someone lost it," she said, inspecting it closely.

I scanned the horizon. Of the 62 islands in these coral atolls, only 17 were inhabited. Many were without electricity, running water, or telephones. *This little dress made quite a journey.*

Running down to the water's edge, Kelsey rinsed and shook the fabric, revealing a faded blue-and-yellow plaid sundress with buttons down the back.

"It's just my size! Can I keep it?" She held it up to her body.

"I don't see why not! Let's take it back to *Ohana* and give it a good washing!"

We will never know the story behind the little dress. Perhaps it came off the lifelines of a boat as it dried in the sun or left on the beach by a little village girl miles away. Whatever the case, it became Kelsey's favorite dress. She wore it often, and it is stored in her "special items" bin to this very day.

Traveling with our girls made us slow down and appreciate these simple days I knew we'd never get back. Through the eyes of our children,

I started appreciating life with a new and genuine curiosity, taking the time to notice and talk about things that once seemed irrelevant.

On *Ohana* the world was ours—we had all we needed and wanted for nothing. With an open mind and a little imagination, we found adventures everywhere. If we look close enough, these special moments are all around us at any time; they are the real treasures.

It is just up to us to find them.

CHAPTER 29

South Pacific Paradise

Vava'u Islands, Tonga

"Oua lau e kafo kae lau e lava."
(Stay positive and count your blessings.)

—TONGAN PROVERB

The following weeks were spent with several buddy boats in Tonga, otherwise known as the Friendly Islands. Our adventurous days in Vava'u marked the end of our sailing journey together before making the jump to New Zealand. Uncertain if we'd ever see each other again, about 30 families would gather on the beach, sharing thoughts about where to go next and what was best for our kids. Oftentimes we'd simply grab our guitars and play. Singing was just easier.

While the men belted out "Brown-Eyed Girl" at the top of their lungs, the women organized a farewell event for the following day, our last in this island paradise. The festivities included a parade of flags, followed by rowing races, coconut toss, an obstacle course, and hermit crab races. Everyone's home country was represented: Norway, England,

Germany, South Africa, Australia, USA, Canada, Ireland, and New Zealand. Paul and the other dads led all the children around the island, each holding their boat's flag as young Tongans happily jumped in line.

All the boat kids, ranging from age three to 14, participated and cheered for their home team. Families from all over the world convened on the shore to celebrate our sailing accomplishments and new friendships that would last a lifetime.

That evening we were invited to a traditional Tongan feast and dancing on the beach.

Bringing gifts to exchange, we met our local hosts, who showed us to our places around a *kaipola*. This 10-foot large mat table was made by splitting a coconut frond down the middle stem with the two halves woven together. We were treated to the common Tongan dish called *lu pulu*, which is a mix of coconut milk, onions, tomatoes, and canned corned beef wrapped and steamed in taro leaves.

After dinner, a large wooden bowl was passed around containing a muddy liquid called kava. We got a quick demonstration from a very large Tongan wearing what looked like one of the mats we were sitting on. When consumed, the pounded or chewed root supposedly offers the body a sense of calm and euphoria. *That sounds kind of nice,* I thought, watching as they slurped the brown water.

While all the kids explored the beach with the Tongan children, the adults got a sample of this customary drink. I looked at Paul, wondering how many people used the same wooden spoon. He shook his head as if to say, "Don't even ask." I quickly took a sip and passed it on. The kava tasted like mushrooms with a hint of dirty sock. The heavy, carved bowl made its way around the table a few times until there was happy banter amongst us and our hosts.

Having more than his fair share, our friend sitting across from us shouted, "I can't feel my legs! Oh my gosh, I can't get up!" He laughed like a drunken sailor. We helped peel him off the ground and onto his feet. The Tongans reassured him that the feeling would wear off in about an hour.

Our evening closed out with a lively Polynesian dance show with all joining in. It was after dark when we finally launched our dinghies off the beach, waving goodbye to our new island friends. Although we would never forget our time in this incredible South Pacific paradise, a whole new adventure was out there waiting for us.

It was time once again to raise our sails and set a course for new horizons.

SECTION 3

Aim

CHAPTER 30

Hang On!

Kermedic Trench, South Pacific

"On the other side of a storm is the strength that comes from having navigated through it. Raise your sail and begin."

—GREGORY S. WILLIAMS

We were forewarned by those who came before us that the passage from Nuku'alofa, Tonga, to New Zealand would most likely be challenging. They were not wrong. Our final 1,100 ocean miles took us from the bucolic trade winds into the higher latitudes where the weather was "friskier," as Paul called it. Generally, we'd sail ahead of the fronts and wait for an opportunity. On our catamaran, we could generally sail at a speed that kept us moving fast enough to outrun a cold front. On this particular route, we were right on the razor's edge for hours and we all hung on for dear life.

Madison would occasionally study my face for any sign of terror whenever our boat slammed into the next wave. Through bared teeth, I smiled at her. "All good, babe!" I hollered above the noise. "Just a little rough patch!" There was no sense making our little crew more anxious than they probably were.

As *Ohana* rose to the peaks, she'd pick up speed, cresting the 60-foot swell and take off down the backside at a breakneck 17 knots. Every time the hulls slammed into the next oncoming wave, I closed my eyes and prayed, *Please God don't let our boat split in two!*

With all the hatches locked up tight, the stuffiness and smell of diesel added to my nausea. The girls were in a "cruising coma" watching *Little House on the Prairie* one episode after another. *What I would give to be Ma Ingalls right now running through a wheat field,* I thought just as a shuddering *kaboom!* shook the entire boat.

"Wow, that was a big one!" Paul said, giving me a reassuring glance. "We'll be out of this soon, honey. You're doing great!" Quieter than usual, I knew that my generally optimistic husband was even a little concerned.

For five agonizing hours, Paul and I stared outwards at each oncoming wave, catching our breath as each one passed. Together we stayed the course, took the hits, and managed to get through it unscathed. The front eventually passed with little drama other than broken glass and a floor full of popcorn kernels that had flung off the shelf.

I welcomed the long and monotonous days, but we were all very tired and ready to make landfall. Everything was encrusted with salt, our bodies sticky, sweaty, and sore from being tossed around like a dryer sheet. We had 600 nautical miles to go and I had pretty much given up on parenting. Madison changed into every outfit she had on board as if she were going to meet the queen. She settled on a velour navy jumpsuit, a purple beanie, and mittens, of course. Kelsey, on the other hand, chose clean pink underwear and remained glued to her movie, *Pocahontas*. I let the princesses take over. I was off duty.

I rummaged around in our cool box, discovering the head of cabbage that had rolled to the back since Suwarrow, amazed at how long it lasted. Adding that to Rice-A-Roni, canned peas, canned chicken, and green beans, I managed to create something that resembled dinner.

Handwashing the dishes in our usual green plastic tub, Paul took the sunset watch, giving me time with the girls. Madison had already jumped in Kelsey's bunk, and I snuggled between them. We created a wall around us with stuffed animals to cushion our bodies from rocking back and forth. Their bare legs flung across mine, securing us to one another. I couldn't help but think, *here we are in the middle of the ocean and right below us is the deepest, darkest water—a whole entire world down there!* How crazy it seemed—the girls and I lying under an orange-and-yellow quilt while just four inches of fiberglass kept us afloat.

I thought about the notion of "home" and what that really meant. After driving 5,000 miles across America and sailing another 9,200 more, home seemed to be wherever my family was.

Staring out at the sky from the above hatch, I felt a pang of melancholy. This chapter was closing. It had just been us, the sea, time, and each other. Selfishly, there was a part of me that didn't want to give this up. I knew we would never be here again, at least not like this.

The sky was overcast; salt had formed in various shapes on the plexiglass as one wave after another washed over our boat. I secured the hatch and settled between them.

That day on the playroom floor felt like a lifetime ago, staring at a map, running my finger down the islands to a place that seemed unreachable. My dream of sailing to New Zealand with my family, my *Ohana*, had come true.

I lay there wondering if the books were accurate. *Were there more sheep than people? Would I learn to like Vegemite and mince pies? Would I be able to drive on the left side of the road? Would I remember how to drive at all?* I felt a chill and pulled the quilt over us. The weather was getting cooler just as predicted. Madison and Kelsey were already fast asleep in my arms. I made a mental note to get out our cold-weather gear I had packed away years ago. Up until now, we hadn't needed it. I kissed them on the forehead and closed my eyes. Three more days at sea.

I wanted to freeze this moment. I thought I was ready, but now I wasn't sure. From the moment we left Alaska, I thought of the many years of unforgettable experiences the four of us shared . . .

Despite that awful storm, I was really going to miss this.

CHAPTER 31

New Zealand

Opua, Bay of Islands, New Zealand

"If you want to buy a slice of Heaven,
you need to make New Zealand your home."

—ROD DONALD

Like marathoners limping across the finish line, we finally motored into the Bay of Islands. We had made it.

"Sheep! Those are sheep!" The girls pointed to the hundreds of little woolly animals grazing on the vibrant green hillsides. So far, the ratio of sheep far outnumbered any humans. Shielding our eyes from the glaring sun, we stood in awe together on the foredeck, taking it all in.

Paul gently motored *Ohana* alongside the quarantine dock. Stepping off the transom onto the concrete pier, I wanted to be first to stand in our new country. Shaking out my sea legs, I jumped up and down with excitement, tying off the dock lines Paul had tossed me. I gazed out at our new surroundings. Slight breeze, clear skies, and seagulls calling overhead. The warmest welcome.

Since it was Sunday, the customs office was closed. We were about to discover pretty much everything closed on Sunday—a day New Zealanders spent with family. We gladly took this day of rest as well. We weren't allowed off our boat until the officials properly checked us in anyway. So, the girls and I jumped on the trampolines while Paul did the usual post-arrival boat check. We danced and stretched the kinks out of our bodies before collapsing across the netting. The girls sprawled out next to me, gazing up at the sky. It was the bluest blue I had ever seen. The clouds looked like airbrushed balloon animals, almost unreal. *Maybe this is why they call New Zealand the "Land of the Long White Cloud,"* I thought, pointing one out that looked like a dragon. Kelsey giggled. She loved dragons.

Propping up on my elbows, I scanned our new environment. The sun reflected bright diamond-shaped sparkles across the water. An old-fashioned dairy sign with the words "Tip Top" hung off a quaint little building on stilts over the shore. A picture of an ice cream cone gave the store an old-fashioned charm. I couldn't wait for the kids to discover this shop as soon as we got off the boat to explore our new town. Squinting, my eyes followed the perimeter of the marina. Our catamaran was amongst the community of ocean-going vessels that found their way into Opua from all corners of the globe. I noticed a ship's chandlery, a club-house decorated with flags, a bakery, a laundromat, and public showers. I couldn't wait to wash the salt out of my hair and stand under hot water again for longer than a minute.

The colorful Optimist dinghies lining the beach waiting for little weekend sailors made me smile. *This couldn't be a more perfect place,* I thought, shaking my head. It was everything I imagined it would be and more.

I wanted to stay forever. *Could this be home?* I wondered, laughing to myself at the thought. We hadn't even gone beyond the marina yet.

Eventually, I crawled into our bunk next to my husband, who had already made his way down to our cabin for a long nap. We lay on top of the damp sheets, too sticky to bother with an extra layer. I had the girls settle down as well. *Ohana*, finally motionless, lay still and steady as the heartbeat in my chest. Taking hold of Paul's hand, I collapsed and fell fast asleep.

Paul and I knew that once we arrived in New Zealand, things would unfold naturally. We were simply happy to turn off the engines for a while. There were times we had thought about circumnavigating and making our way around the world, but like many of our fellow cruising friends, we felt it was time for the kids to have some formal education and experience life in one place for a while. So far, the Bay of Islands looked pretty good to me.

Once we were cleared in and our vast shell collection was thoroughly inspected for unwanted intruders, we were assigned the perfect slip near the ferry terminal with a 360-degree water view. The "last call" horn became our alarm clock as passengers and cars were transported to and from the quaint historic town of Russell and islands beyond.

We spent the following weeks welcoming our cruising friends arriving from Tonga and areas of the Pacific. Scruffy, sore, and happy, they joined us aboard *Ohana*, sharing their harrowing sea stories over several bottles of Steinlagers. Eventually, we all dispersed—some, like ourselves, toured the country first while many settled into various towns on the North and South Islands. A handful of die-hard sailors continued their circumnavigation while others returned to their home countries. For us, it never crossed our minds to go back to Alaska.

We fell in love with New Zealand from the minute we sailed in.

CHAPTER 32

The Scenic Route

Bay of Islands – Wellington, New Zealand

"Don't just tell your children about the world. Show them."

—PENNY WHITEHOUSE

I t was November and summer on this side of the world.

The native Pohutukawa trees burst with gorgeous red blossoms, marking the beginning of the holiday season in the Southern Hemisphere. We rented a camper van, touring the entire North Island for a month before the girls began their first term at school. The tiny recreational vehicle was nowhere near the size of the colossal motorhomes back in the USA, but we quickly realized almost everything here matched the size of the country—small!

With frequent stops in every town, we got to know the culture, understand the customs, and met amazing people along the way. The ever-changing scenery was mind-blowing. Everywhere we turned was like being on the movie set of *The Lord of the Rings*. I could just envision Frodo Baggins walking with his staff across Fiordland National Park smiling and waving. Driving over 1,000 kilometers, we passed rocky headlands, blowholes, wild sand dunes, volcanic mountains, gorges, geysers, and sounds. We tramped through boulder fields and forests dense with canopies of fern-like Ponga trees. We ate our way across the country, stopping for fish and chips and savory pies at quaint roadside cafés. Fresh fruit stands were everywhere. What we didn't buy from the local farmers, we'd pick right off the trees. Feijoas were our favorite.

We were treated to an abundance of unspoiled bounty from the tip of the north to the southernmost city of Wellington, the capital of New Zealand. Eight hundred adventurous miles later, it was time to get out of our rolling home and find a new school for the girls. January marked the beginning of a new term for New Zealanders, and the kids were anxious to make new friends.

We discovered Springbank—a little private country school in the town of Kerikeri, 30 minutes outside of Opua. The girls loved choosing the same outfit every day: a white uniform T-shirt, navy shorts, and optional Birkenstock sandals although bare feet were actually encouraged!

Once we got used to right-hand drive and left side roads, we bought ourselves a couple of cars at an auction in Auckland City. Anxious to drive again, I picked out a Toyota Landcruiser while Paul settled on a sporty BMW M3. Having sailed an average of eight knots for the past three years, he deserved his racing stripes.

Taking turns, we'd drive the girls to and from school, passing sheep, cows, and the occasional tractor along the way. After pick-up from the gate, we would stop for "Hokey Pokey" ice cream at the corner "dairy," or family-owned convenience store. I'd grab a handful of candy or "lollies" charmingly displayed next to the newsstand by the register. New Zealand was stuck in the '70s, and we loved every old-fashioned minute of it.

With Maddi and Kelsey bringing aboard new schoolbooks, projects, sports equipment, and musical instruments, finding space on *Ohana* became a challenge. The day Madison fell overboard with a textbook-heavy backpack was the day we finally considered moving off the boat.

On one of our afterschool walks with the girls, we discovered a house for sale overlooking the bay. Perched on the cliffside, the three-story artist's residence had water views from every window. With a population of 360, Opua had very few homes for sale, especially one so idyllic.

Our evening strolls took us back around to 15 English Bay Road, the "for sale" sign taunting us every time. *Were we ready for homeownership again? Here? In a foreign country?* We loved the proximity to the Bay of Islands, endless hiking trails, the active boating community, and the neighboring tourist town of Paihia. The house also came with a mooring ball, giving us direct access to *Ohana* by way of a trail leading to a private beach. From the deck we would be able to keep an eye on her as well as walk down to our dinghy to get to it. A brick garden path weaved its way from the house to the trailhead below. Purple hydrangeas, pink flowering camellia trees, and native bromeliads spilled out over the walkway leading to a fully stocked koi fishpond. The sound of water trickling through a three-tiered rock fountain greeted us at the front door. As perfect as this house seemed, there was a reason it was still on the market.

The gardens were an overgrown jungle, the house lacked a garage, every single room needed upgrading and it was a remodeling project unlike anything we'd ever done before.

"This has Berger family written all over it!" Paul said enthusiastically. *Maybe we could have the best of both worlds,* I thought, *our sailing life as well as a beach house!*

"Why not? What else do we have going on?" I asked Paul. We all agreed. It was time to live on land for a while. This seemed like the perfect place.

After closing on the sale, we moved off *Ohana*, tied her up, and got right to work.

Each day after dropping the girls off at school, Paul and I would dive right into a mile-long list of remodeling projects. "Here we go again!" We'd say excited to roll up our sleeves and build something together just like the good old days.

However, we struggled to find the tools and equipment we needed. We were used to the large home improvement stores in the United States. Although challenging and expensive, we soon took on the positive kiwi attitude and adapted to what was available.

"You'll be right, mate!" The cashiers would happily shout as we left their shops empty-handed. Sure enough, we always were. We made many friends that year—neighbors and locals who jumped in and helped where they could. New Zealanders were some of the kindest, hard-working, most down-to-earth people in the world.

In between crewing in local regattas and helping coach the girls' Optimist sailing club, Paul and I finished two new bathrooms, built a custom office, and installed hardwood flooring. We painted the interior walls white and the exterior a coastal seafoam blue. We bought a houseful of new furniture and hired a landscaper to help turn our yard into a subtropical garden sanctuary. I laid a new pebble driveway and created a large sea turtle tile mosaic to beautify the concrete patio wall. We even adopted a kitten named "Hobie".

Dirty and exhausted, Paul and I would collapse in lounge chairs on the front deck comparing our bee stings and spider bites. Looking out at our expansive view of the bay, we'd sip our drinks while listening to the sounds of Tui birds in the garden below. It was absolute bliss. With the Bay of Islands out our back door, we had endless sailing adventures with new friends and our families who flew over to visit.

We finally had a place to call "home".

Or so we thought.

CHAPTER 33

Turning the Tide

Northland, New Zealand

"There is a time when we must firmly choose the course we will follow,
or the relentless drift of events will make the decision for us."

—HERBERT V. PROCHNOW

The typhoon took us by surprise.

We received a call that our girls would be stuck in Kerikeri possibly overnight or longer due to a storm that was creating major flooding. My neighbor, who was on carpool duty that day, had already picked up Madison, Kelsey, and her daughter from school. Glennis called me from the road to tell me of her decision to get them before the storm got worse. I was so grateful she thought ahead; however, the torrential rains had already washed out the bridge connecting the town of Paihia to Opua. They could go no further.

Paul, bandaged from recent carpal tunnel surgery on his right hand, called our neighbor Alby, who lived just below us on the beach. As always, our helpful Māori friend had a solution. He made two trips with Paul driving his "tinny," an old aluminum fishing boat, to the Paihia pier to pick up our stranded girls and bring them safely home. With the extreme conditions growing stronger out in the bay, it was precarious and risky to say the least.

Torrential rain and wind were menacing, creating a forceful current no boater should be out in. And then came the urgent emergency phone call warning all hillside residents to gather their belongings and seek shelter immediately at the Opua Cruising Club. As emergency sirens blared in the distance, Paul and I knew we had a choice to make—stay at the club for a few days with others or make a break for the boat.

I looked out at *Ohana* bobbing about like a wine cork. We felt that was where we belonged. It was a tough call, but we had to move . . . fast! A neighbor's home had already slid down the cliff and I had no desire to sleep in a stuffy room packed with people. *Ohana* had all we needed: food, water, and foul-weather gear. We would be safe on her mooring until the storm passed.

I quickly explained the plan to the girls. They stuffed their backpacks with a few toys and clothes. We were heading for the boat.

I never knew the level of strength, courage, and determination I possessed until I became a mother. Having to protect my family that day was the moment I found out what I was truly made of. With adrenaline coursing through my body, I rowed like I had never rowed before in my life. With Paul's hand unusable, I was responsible for getting our family quickly and safely to *Ohana*. As rain pelted us like bullets, I intensely focused on every pull, while Paul barked out directions from the bow like a coxswain for a rowing team. Our wide hulled Walker Bay dinghy wanted to go everywhere but in a straight line. We had misjudged how fast the current was, but there was no going back. We had one chance, and there was no room for error or slowing down. I could sense worry on our girl's faces although they cheered me on. "C'mon, mama, you can do it!" they both yelled, staying clear of my flailing arms.

With only one shot to grab onto the boat, Paul would have to elbow catch the bowsprit stay to keep us in place while I hoisted the kids onto the foredeck. It was a precarious position and without a motor, this was our one attempt to get it right. The powerful four-knot current swirled around us like a vortex ready to sweep us out into the bay. Once I climbed onto the bow with the girls, I held the painter line pulling Paul and the dinghy alongside to the transom.

Exhausted and shook up, we were finally safe inside. We hunkered down for a few days until the storm passed and it was safe to go ashore.

Fortunately, our house was spared from the mudslides that sadly destroyed many others.

The great Northland storm of 2007 was a wake-up call for us. As much as we loved our home, we feared the next storm might not be as forgiving. There were other concerns as well that we put aside in favor of living in this little sailing haven in the Bay of Islands. Work, educational opportunities and a bustling city life called to us. Drives back and forth to Auckland were becoming common as we desired a larger church community, more cultural, entertainment and sporting events, and a social scene that only the big city could offer.

We loved Opua and the people that made us feel so welcome, but we knew this could not be our forever home. There was so much more for us yet to be explored—and we knew it.

After much thought and prayer, we put our beautiful home on the market having just lived in it for two years and moved back onboard *Ohana* once again.

CHAPTER 34

Anchoring

Auckland, New Zealand

"I often found something to delight my eyes and heart,
but never something to replace my homeland."

—FRIEDRICH VON BODENSTEDT

While the countryside offered sheep and silence, Auckland offered people and noise.

As sad as it was to leave the home we built, our new friends and peaceful Opua, we loved and embraced the vibrant waterfront with its upscale restaurants, trendy high-end shops, and world-class hospitality.

While Madison and Kelsey adapted unusually well to Kristin—a prestigious independent K-13 school located on 50 acres of park-like grounds—Paul and I had the task of finding another place to live and look for jobs and volunteer opportunities to keep us busy. Although he continued running the family real estate business from afar, Paul's daily tasks were minimal and he needed more to do. Having been "glued at the hip" day in and day out for years we were both ready for a little breathing room.

After weeks of watching ferryboats come and go from the terminal along Quay Street's historic waterfront, Paul found his calling. With a bit of training, he became a captain for the 80-foot passenger ferry, *Osprey*, running commuting passengers between Auckland and shore cities.

In the meantime, I rented us a small two-bedroom cottage in the quiet beach town of Narrowneck along the North Shore and set up our next home. *Ohana* was docked nearby at Bayswater Marina where we would take her out on weekend trips to Rangitoto Island to explore and hike its dormant volcano. I would often go on my 4 km run to meet the ferry and join Paul on one of his shifts. After school, the girls would volunteer to be the ticket-taker for embarking passengers often getting a chance to "drive" the boat with their dad.

As for me, I joined the triathlon club, became active in church groups, and started a little business of my own. Inspired by the iconic Alaska bike jersey, I created similar designs for New Zealand markets. With the help of Champion apparel, I manufactured and sold my colorful "KiwiJerseys" at various sporting events around the country.

My eye-catching tops made headlines and soon grabbed the attention of the Prime Minister, John Key, as well as a tradeshow booth at the popular Ironman Lake Taupo. I was doing what I loved—meeting new people, participating in races, representing New Zealand, and touring the incredible country I had once dreamed about.

As much as we loved our quaint seaside suburb, we were anxious to get out of our tiny rental and experience more than just rugby, surfing, and sausage rolls. We moved back onboard, sailing *Ohana* over to Auckland's Viaduct Marina, where we were given a slip next to the America's Cup boats. Surrounded by constant activity, our evenings were spent on the bow waving to tourists and enjoying the sights and sounds of city life again.

Between school, theatre, sports, and music, we explored the nearby islands of Motutapu, Motuihe, and Waiheke on the weekends. We moved off the boat once again and into a long-term vacation rental in the trendy suburb of Takapuna. This laid-back, friendly oceanside community had every activity a family could want.

Once we became familiar with our new environment, Paul and I started chartering *Ohana* on the weekends, taking guests out for sunset sails, business gatherings, and special events. For seven incredible years we were blessed to live, play, and work in one of the most beautiful places on earth.

But as picture-perfect as our life was in New Zealand and as hard as we tried, we always knew in the back of our minds, we could never make this country our permanent home. The pull to stay was great, but the necessity to leave was greater.

Our properties back in Alaska deserved our attention. We missed our families and familiar holidays. The girls wanted an American high school experience—homecoming parades, football cheerleading and prom.

Most of all, we wanted a house that didn't move.

CHAPTER 35

Selling Ohana

Auckland, New Zealand

"And suddenly you know:
It's time to start something new and trust the magic of beginnings."

—MEISTER ECKHART

It was a typical chilly day in New Zealand; the overcast skies matched our somber moods as we walked down our pier for the last time to retrieve the rest of our belongings. There she was waiting for us; her lifelines bare except for a couple forgotten clothespins. Our boat had been sold to a young English family.

Ohana seemed so small compared to the megayachts towering over her, but to us, she was the most impressive of them all. Our trusted catamaran had carried us across oceans traveling thousands of miles to countries we otherwise would have never seen in this lifetime. It was time to hand the keys over to a new family ready to begin their own journey.

Stepping off *Ohana* was bittersweet, to say the least. Taking apart what we had put years into. Boat parts, tools, medical equipment, books, food, school projects, clothing, collections, and boxes of shells were packed up, ready to be hauled up the ramp in dock trolleys. Paul was unusually quiet.

"Well, that was fun!" I said trying to lighten things up. He laughed. "Yep, it sure was."

Madison, Kelsey, Paul, and I stretched our arms along its white hulls for a final boat hug. Grabbing the cart handles together, we walked down the dock, turning back for one last glimpse.

"Goodbye *Ohana*! We will never forget you!" The girls shouted before chasing each other up the ramp. Our frayed American flag, still tied to the shroud, waved in the breeze. We left it there as a token—a reminder of where we came from and the freedom it represented—life, liberty, and the pursuit of happiness. We had been blessed with all three.

It was the end of a dream but the beginning of a new one.

It was time to go home.

CHAPTER 36

Home

Anchorage, Alaska

"We shall not cease from exploration, and the end of all our exploring will be to arrive where we started and know the place for the very first time."

—T. S. ELIOT

There it was. Our shipping container had arrived. New Zealand in a box.

A month earlier, Madison and I had flown back to Alaska to look at properties for sale. Our soon-to-be-freshman wanted to see her new school and would help me pick out our new home. There was no need for Paul and Kelsey to join us on the 15-hour flight if we had no luck.

With the help of our realtor friend, Carole found us a five-bedroom home on an acre lot near the mountains yet close enough for the girls to bike to school. Our offer was accepted.

We returned to Auckland to pack up our things and say goodbye to many of our dear friends, the hardest part of all.

Finally, the four of us stepped off the plane at Anchorage International Airport. The familiar sights and Alaskan souvenir shops were a welcome comfort. The huge taxidermy moose greeted us at the gate. People in XtraTuf boots and camo jackets lined the baggage claim, waiting for their empty coolers that would soon be filled with freshly caught salmon. We were back.

Dragging our bags behind us, we were finally walking to the front door of our new house. Cottonwood seeds peppered the path like confetti. I stopped briefly to close my eyes, inhaling the fresh air—wild, beautiful Alaska.

We took the summer to unpack, decorate our new home, and enrolled the girls in sports and music camps. We wanted to give them as much time as possible to socialize before they jumped into middle and high school.

The first year was challenging for both Madison and Kelsey. Their homeschool and overseas learning environments were very different from the public education system in America. They had just come from a prestigious campus where cricket was played during recess, blazers and ties were mandatory, and Mandarin was the language of choice. They weren't sure how or where to fit in.

I empathized with our teenagers and the many changes they faced but living and traveling on a boat had taught them to be resilient and brave. I knew that with every heartache they had an opportunity to grow. We had equipped our daughters with a worldview far beyond what many kids would ever experience. We had taught them to adapt to a world of uncertainty, but more importantly, to put their faith in God and trust the journey.

The following years proved to be tough, but they persevered. Soon Madison emerged from eating lunch alone in the bathroom stall to becoming Homecoming Queen, cheerleading captain, and standout singer in swing choir. Meanwhile, Kelsey customized her education to suit her. With a wide range of charter schools to choose from, she excelled academically and creatively through courses that inspired her artistic talents. She went on to become yearbook editor, varsity tennis player, and the youngest designer at one of Alaska's leading graphic design companies.

As for Paul and me, life back in our hometown hadn't changed much. The only difference was us. I felt like we had lived a secret life together and trying to explain our 10-year sabbatical to others was nearly impossible.

"What? You just bought a boat and sailed away?" Our new friends would ask until the conversation drifted back to football scores and the weather. Understandably so, I had a hard time making sense of it all myself.

"You should write a book about it!" They encouraged me.

Someday, maybe, I thought.

Paul jumped right back into managing our properties, making long-overdue upgrades to our existing apartment buildings, and checking in with the tenants. We were so fortunate to have dedicated managers that gave us the freedom to travel. We could not have lived out our dream without them.

I, on the other hand, had been diagnosed with Atrial fibrillation (Afib) our final year in New Zealand which resulted in emergency heart surgery upon returning to Alaska. After a successful ablation procedure, I exchanged my highly aerobic lifestyle in favor of a more balanced one. It wasn't easy, but I knew God had a plan for me in this new season. Encouraged by my friend Katey, owner of Anchorage Yoga, I started taking classes and realized the physical and healing power of yoga. I learned how to control my breathing, the importance of meditation and flowing rather than fighting against change. This new mindset helped me embrace the move back to Alaska—to experience a whole new life I had left long ago with renewed energy and purpose.

Our house soon filled up with trinkets from our travels and the energetic chatter of old and new friends. It didn't take long before we were right back where we started—a houseful of furniture, hot showers, stainless-steel appliances, and luxurious king-size beds. I fell back in love with the familiar city I grew up in, the mountains, lakes, and my favorite scenic drive along the Turnagain Arm. I began to enjoy Alaska again for what it was rather than what it wasn't. It was my home, a place to return to, not escape from.

I appreciated the littlest things having traveled halfway around the world to feel content right where I was. Most importantly, we experienced every facet of our children growing up while living out our dream together—the greatest gift of all.

Knowing there was a very small window of opportunity during their teenage years, we spontaneously bought another sailboat, christening her the *Ohana 2*. Paul found the 40-foot Hunter in New England with the sole intention of father-daughter trips before they graduated high school—a significant decision that created a lifelong bond between them.

Madison, age 16, along with her dad, sailed from Annapolis, Maryland delivering it up the coast to Mystic, Connecticut, while Kelsey, age 13, took the helm from Stonington, and together sailed up to Martha's Vineyard and Nantucket.

Sure enough, Maddi got engaged a few years later to a wonderful young man she met after graduating high school. She and her dad shared a sailing trip to the Bahamas with her fiancé before the *Ohana 2* was sold. It was a very narrow window indeed.

Currently, Madison and her husband, Elliott, are successful business owners in Scottsdale, Arizona. Our little entrepreneur selling seashells and doing nail art and makeovers as a child went on to launch her own beauty business—Light Heart Studios and Coffee Shop. She is an award-winning educator, podcaster, and speaker. People come from all over the world to take her courses, receive beauty services, and enjoy gourmet coffee at their popular café.

Kelsey, our little artist who repurposed beach glass and sold pet rocks as a child, went on to study at Auckland's Whitecliffe College of Arts and Design on her returning resident's visa. After receiving her Certificate in Fine Arts, she traveled to Japan on a language and cultural exchange, obtained her real estate license, and currently works as an administrator and graphic designer. She and her boyfriend, Reese, are about to go on their first road trip. Surely, one of many.

This was our mission, to see that our girls were raised with the tools necessary to pursue their dreams and make their own way. Most importantly, to live authentically with solid moral values, to love what they do while making the world a better place.

They have far exceeded our expectations.

Paul and I continue to navigate life as empty nesters, extending our collection of investment properties to include a historic bar, The Carousel Lounge, a coffee business, and a couple of Airbnb's. Our wanderlust has been replaced with new adventures right outside our back door.

As I write, my husband is waxing the hull of an old Bayliner in our backyard. Until it's time for our forever boat, this little motor yacht will satisfy our love of the water right here in Alaska's Prince William Sound.

It has taken me years to finish this book while life swirls around me like that fast-moving current. This time I'm flowing with it. It has been my goal to not only preserve but share our story with my family and those wishing to live life to the fullest, to live out their dreams, whatever they may be.

Having sailed to 18 different countries and moving eight times over the course of ten years, I now find myself right back where I started, only this time seeing everything completely different. My heart is open, my eyes lifted, and my spirit content. By leaving Alaska, I discovered for myself who I was as a mother, wife, daughter, sister, and friend.

The beauty of writing was that I was able to relive that incredible chapter all over again, years upon years of cherished moments.

As the words poured out and onto these pages, I felt the warmth of the sun-drenched islands and the wind in my hair. I heard the laughter of our children running barefoot along a sandy shoreline and the sound of a faraway conch shell at sunset. I heard the cry of seagulls at first sight of land and felt my husband's arms around me as we took the helm of our ship together.

Get a map. Have a dream. Go on a journey.

Write your story.

Acknowledgments

Without the love and support of my parents, Betty and Daniel Deering, I could never have lived the life I described in these pages. I am in awe of your courage and trust in me to follow my heart and raise our children unconventionally on the opposite side of the world.

Thank you, Donna and Richard Berger, for your enthusiasm and willingness to hop a plane on a moment's notice to come visit us in Alaska, Tahiti, Bahamas, the Virgin Islands, and New Zealand. Your laughter was heard across the Pacific.

To my sister Susie and family who shared many incredible sails with us throughout Fiji and the Bay of Islands. Our adventurous days searching for the perfect shells will never be forgotten.

To my sister Allison, Ironman triathlete and cancer survivor, you inspire me to do more than just finish, but finish well. And to her husband, Scott, for flying across the world to help steer us back on course.

Every good story starts with a great introduction, and I have Armand Nyborg to thank for that!

Shout out to my friend, Scotti Steele, my one and only beta-reader. Your fresh perspective and encouragement kept me sailing along smoothly!

Here's to our friendSHIPS: *LaNovia, SeaFever, Wanderer, 3T, Moonshadow, Bump, Ocean Breezes, Glass Slipper, Wetnose, Rio Dulce, Dare, Dawn Treader* and the many others that were a huge part of our sailing story and still friends with to this day.

Janice and Anthony Thorpe, thank you for inviting my restless husband to crew with you on *Moxie* in the Atlantic Rally for Cruisers. That epic experience should hold him over until we get back on board again!

Madison, with your tenacity and success in beautifying the world "one lash at a time", you have inspired and reignited my passion to continue to do the things that bring me joy. Thank you for always cheering me to the finish line!

Kelsey, hopefully you will have a better recollection of your seafaring childhood after reading this. Your curiosity and love for all people and different cultures have opened my heart and enriched my life in the process. Thank you for your creative input as well as encouragement. "I believe in you, Mom" are treasured words that kept me writing!

Most of all I want to thank my husband and best friend, Paul Berger. Thank you for being the visionary that you are, for believing in my dreams and for your faith in me to share our story.

Rᴇʙᴇᴄᴄᴀ "Bᴇᴄᴋʏ" Bᴇʀɢᴇʀ was born and raised in Anchorage, Alaska.

She holds a bachelor's degree in communication studies from the University of Nevada, Las Vegas where she studied journalism and public relations.

Although Becky has had careers in advertising, retail, hospitality, and the airline industry, her most rewarding role is being a mother of two extraordinary daughters, Madison and Kelsey.

When she's not traveling and working with her husband Paul, Becky enjoys teaching yoga, hosting Airbnb guests, boating, hiking, writing, and spending quality time with family and friends.